friendship
FORGED in FIRE

British Ceramics in America

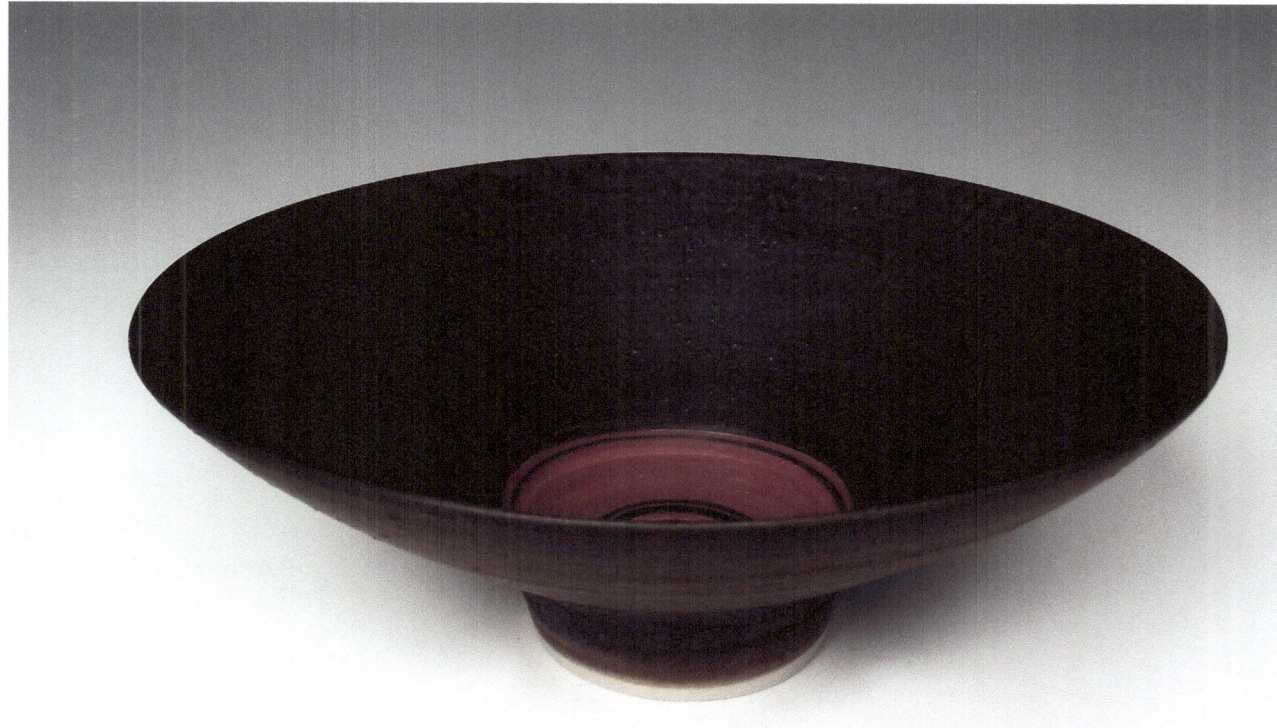

Lucie Rie, (1902-1995)
Flared Bowl, 20th Century
AMOCA Permanent Collection,
Gift of the Estate of Rayona Brenden

Co-Curated by Richard Jacobs and Christy Johnson
Essays by Richard Jacobs
Photography: Nicole Frazer
Layout Design: Susan Reed

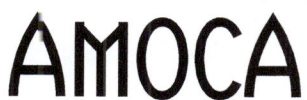

American Museum of Ceramic Art

AMOCA

COPYRIGHT

Published by
The American Museum of Ceramic Art
399 N. Garey Avenue
Pomona, CA 91767
www.amoca.org
1-909-865-3146

AMOCA Founder: David Armstrong
Director & Curator: Christy Johnson
Staff: Rody N. López, Associate Curator; Nicole Frazer, Collection Manager; Angie Reyes, Associate Curator of Education; Susan Reed, Communication & Marketing Manager; Victor Crosetti, Membership Coordinator; Tina Vega, Guest Services; Danika Jensen, Collections Intern.

Essayist: Richard Jacobs
Catalog Design by Susan Reed
Photography Credits: Nicole Frazer
Editing: Julianne Armstrong and Milton Wilson

Text font: Calibri and Myriad Pro

Cover: Lucie Rie (1902 - 1995), *Bottle*, c. 20 AMOCA Permanent Collection Gift of Bill Burke

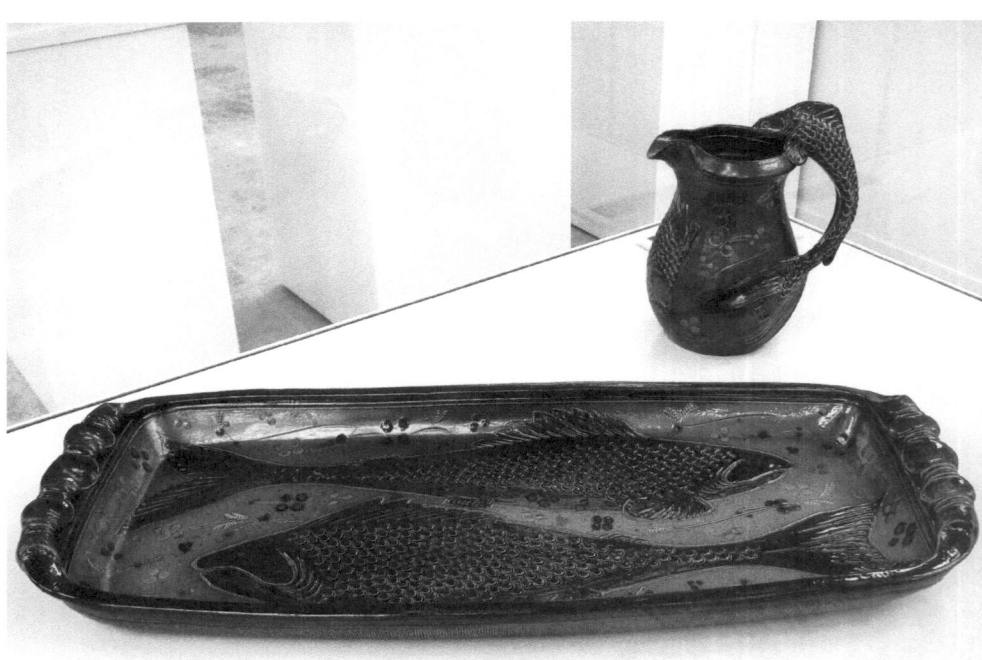

Toff Milway, (b. 1949)
Pitcher and Tray, 20th Century
Collection of Kent Tool

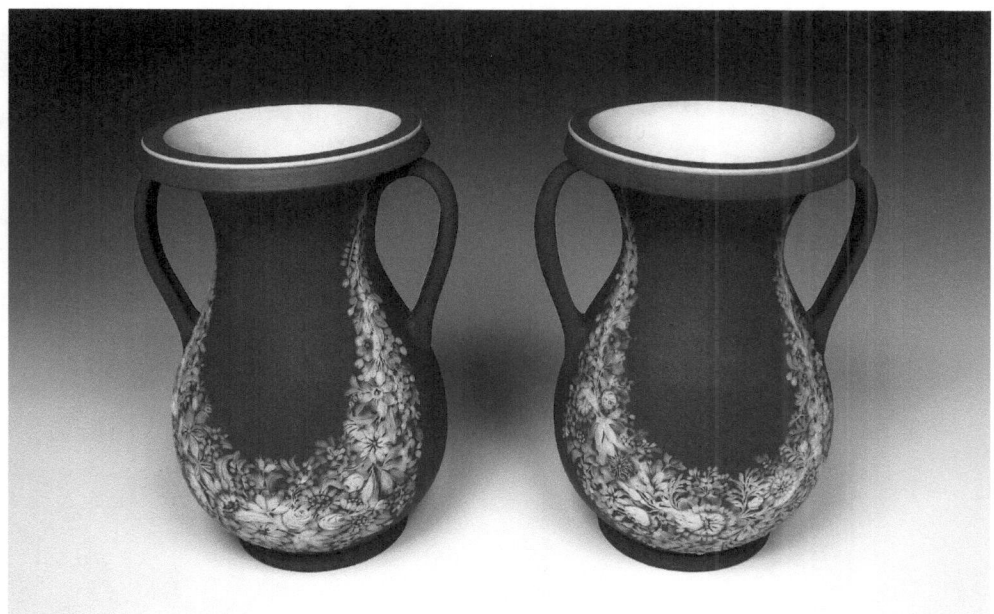

Jaspar Dip Slip Decoration Vases, c. 1878-1880
Wedgwood, Designed by
Fedeick A. Rhead
Courtesy of the Wedgwood
Society of Southern California

CONTENTS

4 **Dedication**: Remembering Bill Burke

5 **Acknowledgments**

6 **Lenders and Artists**

7 **Historical Legacy:** The Great 19th Century Victorian Industrial Potteries

12 **British Culture and Ceramics:** Have a Cuppa Tea?

14 **The Domestic Interior:** The Heartland of the British Arts and Crafts Movement

16 **Worldwide Influence:** The Role of British Ceramics in the Arts & Crafts Movement

19 **The British Studio Art Potter:** The Struggle Between Tradition and Modernism in the 20th Century

27 **The Cultural Impact of Modernism:** Loss of Innocence or the Triumph of Sophistication?

30 **Postmodern British Ceramics:** Can New Meanings and Objects be Created Out of the Meanings and Objects of the Past?

34 **Catalogue**

DEDICATION: REMEMBERING BILL BURKE

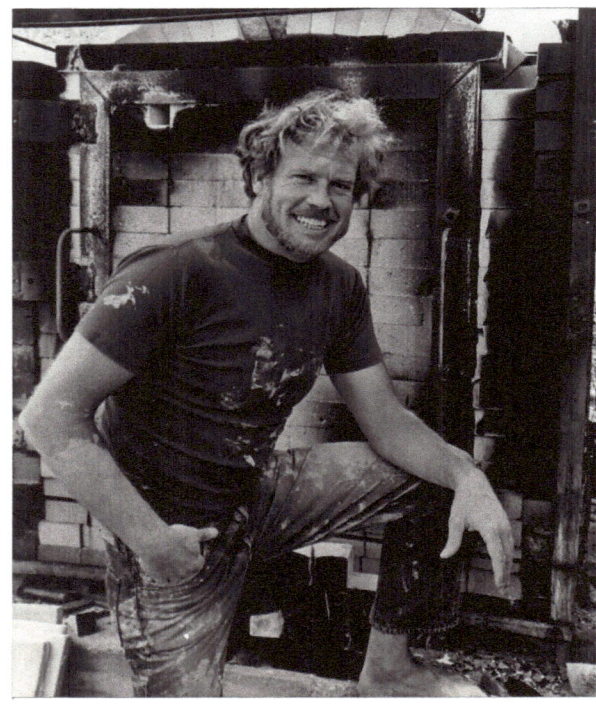

Bill Burke (1935-2009)

AMOCA's collection is an amazing resource. To increase the visibility of the collections, the museum seeks to incorporate the work into its exhibitions. A British exhibit was proposed, highlighting a portion of AMOCA's collection which was gifted by Bill Burke in 2009

Bill Burke was a ceramic artist and collector living in the bay area. A major part of his collection represents San Francisco artists, many of whom were his close friends. Beyond his local community, Bill Burke collected British pottery. He recalled the times he traveled to Britain, met the artists, and purchased pottery. Several of the Lucie Rie pieces on view were a personal gifts to Bill, handed to him by Lucie. His collection includes works by Hans Coper, Lucie Rie, Geoffrey Swindell, Duncan Ross, John Ward, Richard Batterham, Phil Rogers, and David Leach. Thirty pieces from the Burke Collection are presented in this exhibit, including six exquisite Lucie Rie forms.

Bill Burke passed away in 2009, just after donating his collection. We thank him for entrusting the Museum with his valuable collection. His legacy has continued through AMOCA's exhibitions and programming over the past three years.

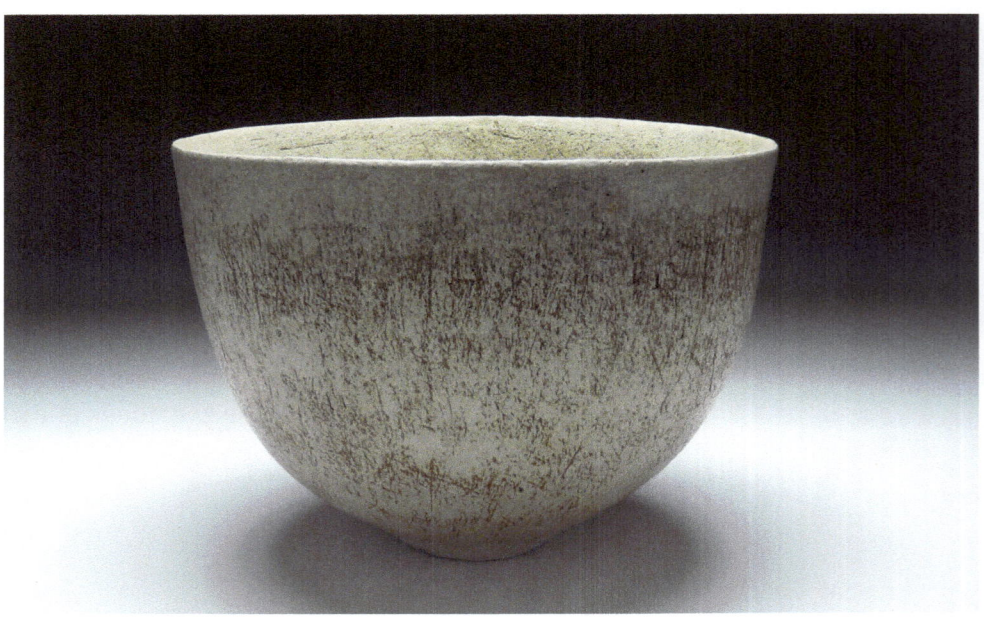

John Ward, (b. 1938)
Bowl, 20th Century
AMOCA Permanent Collection, Gift of
Bill Burke

ACKNOWLEDGMENTS

At the top of the acknowledgement list is the name Armstrong, and not just because it begins with the first letter of the alphabet, but because David Armstrong, Founder of the American Museum of Ceramic Art, and his wife Julianne, provide active leadership and powerful inspiration. The gratitude expressed here for Armstrong's support of this exhibition and for their overall support of AMOCA, both physically and financially, cannot be overstated. They are the soul of AMOCA and an irreplaceable asset of the ceramic community.

Friendships Forged in Fire: British Ceramics in America takes a winding journey though British ceramic history, beginning with ceramics that illustrate the Victorian Era and the Arts and Crafts Movement, moving to examples rooted in Bernard Leach's "ethical-pot" fundamentalism, the post-WWII age of "modernism," and finishing with vast variations of "post-modern" contemporary ceramic art. As applicable to British ceramics or even more broadly to global ceramics, this exhibit purports to encourage the viewer to weigh the experimental climate of current cultural expression against traditional definitions of beauty and mastery of skills.

The inspiration for this exhibit began with a gift of contemporary British ceramics donated to AMOCA in 2010. The works belonged to William Burke, a collector and avid potter. Burke left his collection to the museum along with a generous unrestricted fund. I also want to express my gratitude to John Toki who originally connected Burke with AMOCA and to Kent Tool who, prior to becoming an AMOCA Board member, acted as the facilitator and executor for the Burke gift.

Local collector, Richard Jacobs, who traveled to England for many extended visits and who owns many British works, reviewed AMOCA's plan for a British exhibit and enthusiastically joined the effort. He conceived the general organization of the show and wrote about the history and philosophies of the various eras. We owe Jacobs a debt of gratitude for his guidance and loans as well as his essays which appear in this publication. Above all, I should note Jacob's generous spirit, having donated his time to this project without compensation.

At the crux of making this exhibit possible are the lenders, individuals and institutions who entrusted their precious and valuable works to AMOCA for the duration of the exhibit: Cyndi Andrews, David & Julianne Armstrong, Carolyn & Sam Black, Sharon & Paul Dauer, Judy & Richard Jacobs, Jason Jacques Gallery, Norman Karlson, Hannah & Russel Kully, Jo Lauria & Michael Fargo, Lynn Myers, Carol Pierce, Marcella Ruble, Heather & Chris Rupp, Scripps College, Diane & Igal Silber, Kent Tool, Robert Wedgwood, and Members of the Wedgwood Society of Southern California. For their generosity, we are deeply grateful; without their benevolence there would be no exhibit. I also want to acknowledge those who played a role in connecting AMOCA to resources: Frank Lloyd, Jeffrey Spahn, Jo Lauria, and Michael Smith of the Wedgwood Society. Special thanks to ceramic artists Gareth Mason and Steven Dixon for their participation in demonstration and public participation programs related to this exhibition.

Christy Johnson
AMOCA Director

LENDERS

Cyndi Andrews
David & Julianne Armstrong
Carolyn & Sam Black
Sharon & Paul Dauer
Judy & Richard Jacobs
Jason Jacques Gallery
Norman Karlson
Hannah & Russel Kully
Jo Lauria & Michael Fargo
Lynn Myers

Carol Pierce
Marcella Ruble
Heather & Chris Rupp
Scripps College
Diane & Igal Silber
Kent Tool
Robert Wedgwood
Members of the Wedgwood
  Society of Southern California

ARTISTS

Duncan Ayscough
Gordon Baldwin
Richard Batterham
Svend Bayer
Peter Beard
Betty Blandino
Alison Britton
Alan Caiger-Smith
Michael Cardew
Seth Cardew
Michael Casson
Joanna Constantinidis
Emmanuel Cooper
Hans Coper
Jill Crowley
William De Morgan
Marianne De Trey
Michael Dodd
Ruth Duckworth
Ken Eastman
Ray Finch
Linda Gunn-Russell
Shoji Hamada
Peter Hayes

Regina Heinz
Ewen Henderson
Terri Holman
Nicholas Homoky
Joanna Howells
Glynn Hugo
Ann James
Christine Jones
Walter Keeler
Peter Lane
Bernard Leach
David Leach
Jennifer Lee
Thomas Lochhead
Dameon Lynn
William Marshall
Gareth Mason
Toff Milway
Michael Moore
Susan Nemeth
Magdalena Odundo
Elspeth Owen
Colin Pearson
Henry Pim

Sara Radstone
Elizabeth Raeburn
Lucie Rie
Mary Rogers
Phil Rogers
Jim Malone
Duncan Ross
Micki Schloessingk
Martin Smith
Angus Suttie
Geoffrey Swindell
Judy Trim
Ruthanne Tudball
Angela Verdon
John Ward
Peter Wills

Industrial Art By:
Minton
Royal Doulton
Royal Worcestor
Wedgwood

Historical Legacy: The Great 19th Century Victorian Industrial Potteries

By Dr. Richard Jacobs
California Collector of Ceramics

The industrialization of Great Britain that gained momentum in the mid-eighteenth century and continued in the 19th century provided this small nation the resources to expand and obtain a worldwide empire. This had far-reaching impact on the expansion and quality of British pottery making. A very practical and commercially valuable result from this increasing prosperity was the fact that extensive pottery collections were not only accessible to the aristocracy as they had been in the past but were also available to the wealthy industrialists as well as an emerging middle class. Technological improvements allowed more refined, durable and aesthetically pleasing ceramic tableware. Ceramic ware was not limited to the kitchen and dining table but also was widely used in the improvements in what previously had been deplorable sanitary conditions that had impacted the health of communities and the growing populations of metropolitan areas. Ceramic pipe played a vital role in these improvements. There was a wide range of industrial applications for ceramic materials. It was a time of great optimism, of great wealth and yet great poverty in Britain. Paraphrasing Charles Dickens, it was the best of times for the aristocracy and the wealthy industrialists and it was the worst of times for that formerly rural population drawn into the great and growing manufacturing cities of the midlands and who labored in the grimy factories under the most harsh conditions. The emerging middle class eventually became the main market for ceramics in a rapidly expanding economy.

The rigid class system that was once dependent on royal station and a landed aristocracy with their great estate houses expanded to include wealthy industrialists. This was reflected in the ceramic ware that was

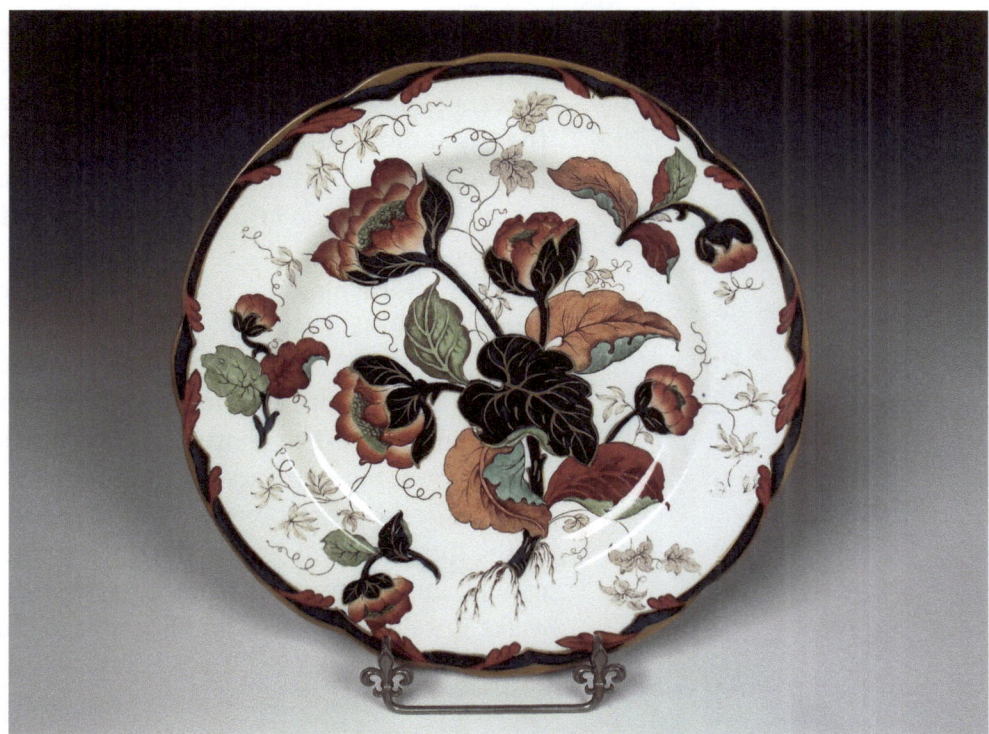

Wedgwood
Water Nymph Plate,
c. 1895
Courtesy of the Wedgwood Society
of Southern California

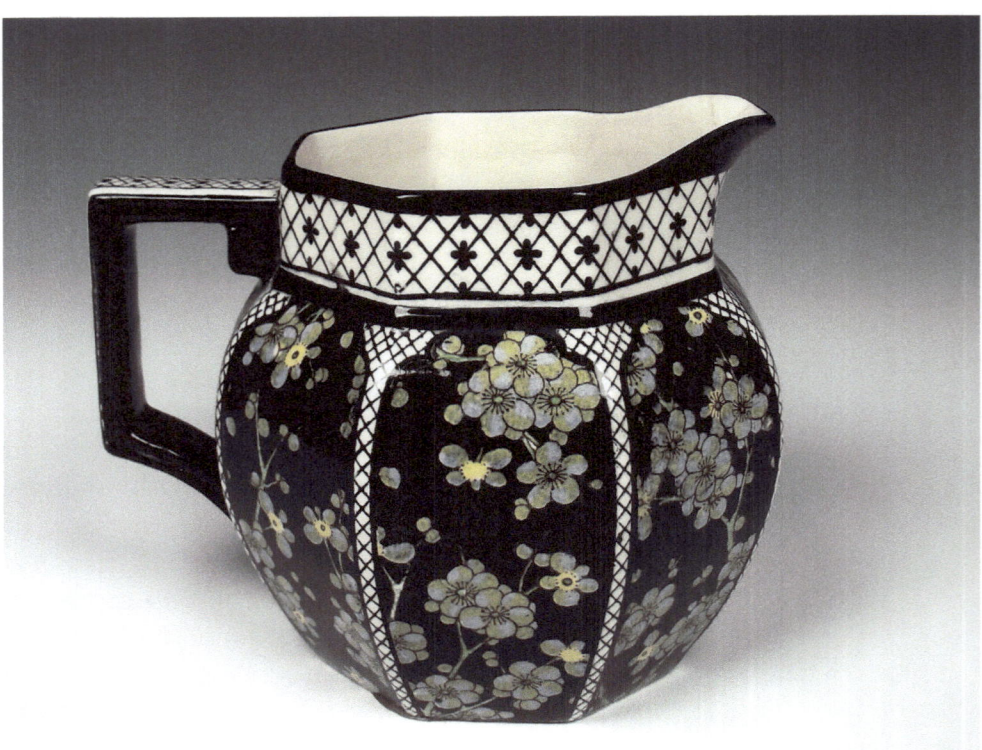

Royal Doulton Jug
Late 19th Century
Collection of Judy &
Richard Jacobs

found in this kind of hierarchical society. Traditional brown stonewares were still available for food storage purposes in taverns as well as the working class domestic kitchen, but there was also a growing market for more decorative fine stonewares that provided more elaborate objects in unusual and intricate shapes. The benefits of the industrialization of pottery making provided inexpensive ceramic ware, practical and useful, created in vast numbers. This required the standardization of the ceramic product while also devising specialized duties for those workers who divided up the various tasks necessary to complete the production of multiples of each object. Aside from the big potteries such as Wedgwood and Royal Doulton, enterprising potters in local regions were able to make a living by supplying the expanding market for ceramic products. Their more modest enterprises allowed more personalized and individually created ceramic wares that would later develop into the studio art potter enterprise.

North Staffordshire and the area around Stoke-on-Trent became one of the largest ceramic manufacturing centers in the country and one of the most influential in the world. This area became known as the Potteries and it is here that over three hundred pottery works had been established by the beginning of the 19th century. Under the leadership and guidance of Josiah Wedgwood, his pottery developed cream-colored earthenware, which was a major departure from the hand-made red earthenware produced by many of the local potters. The leadership of Wedgwood contributed greatly to the conversion of ceramics from a handicraft to a progressive industry and to make Britain the international leader in the production of earthenwares and decorative stonewares. He was not only a giant in the ceramics industry but a pioneer of the Industrial Revolution and one of the most influential leaders of 18th century Britain; known also for his contributions to the fields of history and science, he was also a champion of progressive business practices, including being an early social reformer advocating the abolition of the slave trade. He created the first modern ceramics factory in history. He had a visionary grasp that mass production of pottery would allow the growing middle class to enjoy what was formerly only available for the wealthy. In 1783, Wedgwood became a Fellow of the Royal Society. Nineteenth-century British pottery production became pre-eminent in the field of functional, hardwearing and decorative tableware. The development of large-sized industrial ceramic enterprises was often dependent on founder-leaders such as Wedgwood. Another example was Josiah Spode who ran his own factory in Stoke-on-Trent during the 18th century. Thomas Minton soon became a rival with his own firm, making low-cost, high-quality tableware. He also started to export to America. At the same time the decoration became more lavishly ornate.

The ceramic manufacturer Henry Doulton, son of the founder of the firm, John Doulton, was able to respond to the need for ceramic pipes for drainage and sanitation and his firm was a leader in this field. The passing of the 1848 Public Health Act was in response to repeated outbreaks of cholera and the crisis in public health in Britain. Doulton also produced other sanitary furniture, including stoneware water closets and the world's first stoneware sink, all of which represented major improvements in sanitary technology replacing earlier unhygienic systems of soil removal. Later, clean water could be pumped under pressure using ceramic pipes, first available only to the wealthy, leading to the installment of bathrooms and lavatories within houses. Clay as a fired material was a vital factor in improving public health in the Victorian Age. The fact that the functional and aesthetic evolution of pottery proceeded hand in hand with improvements in the essential living conditions and quality of life for the entire population is surely a proud legacy. Perhaps a few contemporary ceramic artists might be a bit embarrassed to admit the deceptively close historical link between their artistic medium of clay and the arena of public health and sanitation.

In addition to its industrial products, Doulton was able to produce large quantities of high-quality tableware, as well as a range of pieces including teapots and hunting jugs. In the 1860s, Doulton embraced the concept of 'art pottery' and engaged potters who were allowed to initial their work on the bottom of the vase or pot. Some of these potters became well-known designers and ceramic artists even though they continued to function within a factory system. Henry Doulton became the first potter ever to receive the honor of being knighted by Queen Victoria, and in 1901 Edward VII conferred on the company the royal warrant, giving it specific authority to use the name Royal Doulton. Clay's value is apparent in its myriad applications and transformations, ranging from sanitation pipes and toilet facilities to the aesthetic elegance of gracing the dining room tables of the great castles and estate houses of the aristocracy. Clay's historical use in Britain provides a tribute to the importance of clay, as both an applied industrial material and as the very stuff of great ceramic art.

As with other inventions that gave great impetus to the industrialization in Britain, there were similar inventions in British ceramic production and in the technology so important to the industrial process. Among the most significant of these innovations was the continuing experimentation in compositions of clay that provided great improvements in the production of fine quality British pottery. One such example is the porcelain known as bone china. The Spodes were responsible for the expanded commercial use of bone china paste. This paste was further refined, and, although prior to this, British porcelain was thought to be inferior to the porcelain of China and Germany, continued improvements led to the fact that after 1825 nearly all British porcelain was produced in bone china and Britain remained the leader in this field throughout the 19th century. The manufacturers of bone china encouraged the idea of unique porcelain objects that soon became known as 'cabinet pieces' that were created solely for aesthetic contemplation. What set them apart was the skill and talent of the porcelain painter. These special objects, including cups and saucers, were not meant to be used but only admired. By the middle of the 19th century, the china cabinet was an essential item of furniture in almost every middle-class British home.

There was a multiplicity of influences on British industrial pottery during the 19th century, and surges and declines of such influences frequently occurred during the century. Each would attain great popularity and impact but would eventually wane and decline with the appearance of yet another fashionable passion in taste. What was known as the 'Orient' was one such influence. It continued to be a major source for design inspiration during the second half of the nineteenth century. The vast popularity of the blue and

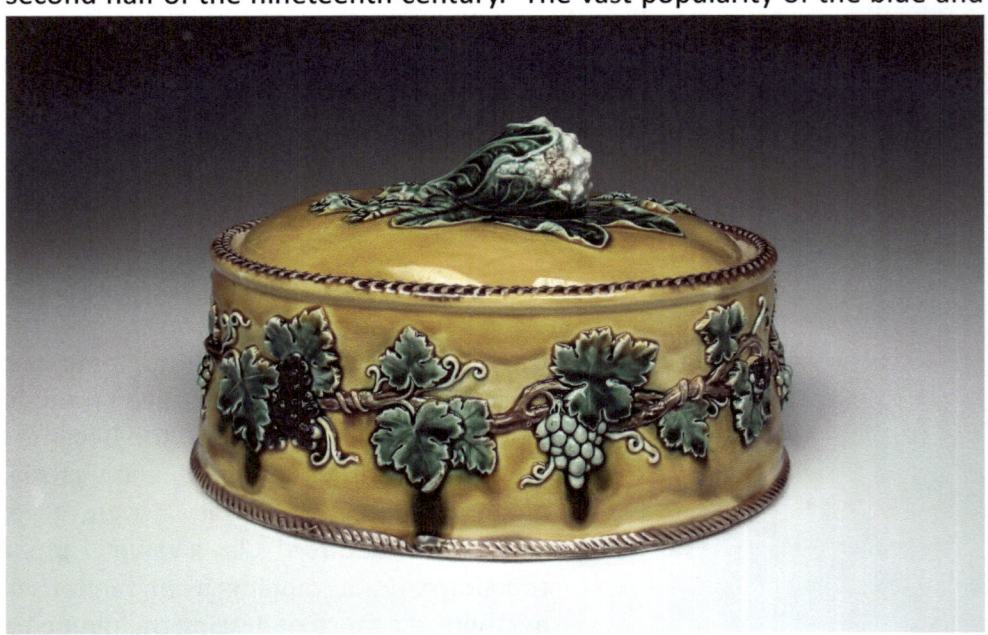

Wedgwood
Majolica Game Pot, 1888
Collection of Cyndi Andrews

white 'Willow' patterned dinnerware is one example. Imari patterns, also known as 'Japan style' were another example of a more general interest in all things *Japonaiserie*.

After the opening of Japan by the West in mid-century, the West was soon flooded with Japanese exports that influenced all the arts and crafts, including ceramic ware.

The Aesthetic Movement of the second-half of the 19th century in Britain espoused an 'art for art's sake' philosophy that rejected the notion that art should serve a social or moral purpose. It influenced Victorian design and impacted the major potteries. It encouraged a rather flamboyant decorative sense that had no function except to delight the eye and bring pleasure to the beholder. The Aesthetic Movement also represented a romanticism that gave increased status to the potter as artist. It was a bit too exotic for British tastes and had a rather brief history there. Pottery in general was elevated in this idealization of these magical manipulations of earth, fire and water that these masters of clay achieved in creating their stunning works.

As the 19th century ended, at the height of their cultural and commercial power, these great industrial potteries were prosperous and prestigious firms that served the British people at the height of this nation's recognized and respected power in the world. Britain at the end of the century enjoyed the benefits derived from the dynamic nature of technological advances and how it could advance the welfare and social progress of a nation. The cultural and economic contributions of ceramics were one of the great gifts of that progress in 19th century Britain.

Royal Worcestor
Scroll-handled Covered Jar, 1892
AMOCA Permanent Collection,
Gift of Robert & Colette Wilson

Royal Doulton
Burslem Biscuit Jar, 1881-1892
Collection of Judy
& Richard Jacobs

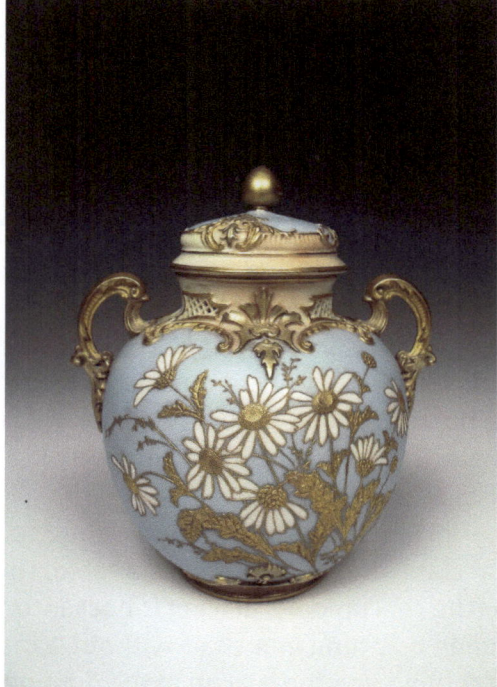
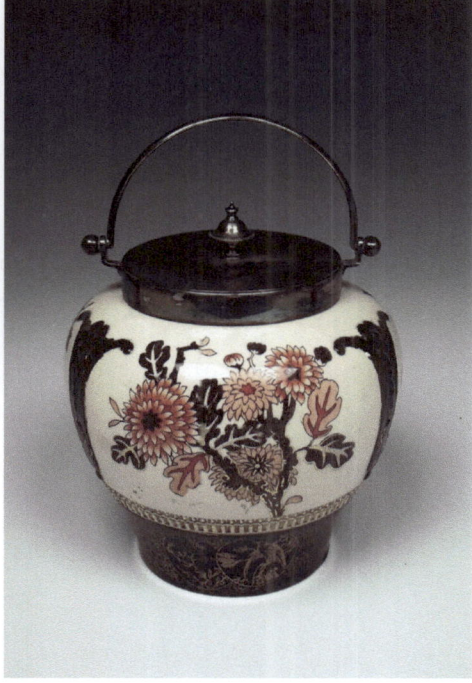

BRITISH CULTURE AND CERAMICS: HAVE A CUPPA TEA?

By Dr. Richard Jacobs
California Collector of Ceramics

The daily use of the tea set, including the ceramic assemblage of teapot, cups and saucers, as well the creamer and sugar bowls, was and still is one of the most beloved British rituals at all levels of society. Since the 18th century, the United Kingdom has been the largest per capita tea consumer in the world. British commercial interests controlled tea production in British India and exported it to Britain in ever expanding amounts. While tea was largely an upper-class drink in Europe, the drinking of tea in Great Britain became an honored and much valued experience of every class. It might well be considered the national tonic of Britain, beloved for the particular leaves of various tea plants from different regions of the world. It was a most welcome hot beverage on the chronically cold rainy days of the notoriously fickle British weather. Tea was also a cultural and individual morale booster, savored and appreciated as allowing timely breaks in the day for all people whatever their station in life and whatever their circumstances. It allowed the entire populace the luxury of a break in their work schedules or household chores. The tea break is the national self-indulgence of the nation whose energy and industry built one of the greatest empires the world has ever seen. However history and habits change things, tea dirinking still is a vital and valued experience for the vast majority of the population.

In Britain tea is usually black tea served with milk (never cream) and sugar for those who desire it a bit sweet. There is a wide array of savories and sweets that accompany tea. A cream tea is clotted cream served on scones, usually with strawberry jam, a tradition. One does not usually restrict oneself to a single cup; often people drink up to six or more cups a day. Employers generally allow breaks for tea. The drinking of tea and the time allocated for such activity was perceived and defined as a central right of all freedom loving Britons.

Ceramics specially designed to facilitate the drinking of tea go back to the 1660s. Small porcelain tea bowls were used by the fashionable. Tea drinking motivated the search for a European imitation of Chinese porcelain, first successfully produced in England in the late 18th century. Tea had been quite expensive at first, but from the late 19th century it dropped in price and remained relatively low throughout the first half of the 20th century. The demand increased for teacups, pots and dishes to go along with the popular new drink. It is a matter of cultural interest that in China the teacups had no handles. However, this did not suit the British and their teacups do indeed have handles. The production of ceramic tea sets was a central factor in the growth of the British ceramic industry in the 19th century.

The drinking of tea had its own etiquette, more elaborate as one ascended social class. If one is seated at a table, the proper manner to drink tea is to raise the teacup only, placing it back into the saucer in between sips. When standing or sitting in a chair without a table, one holds the tea saucer with the off hand and the teacup in the dominant hand. The teacup should never be held or waved in the air. Fingers should curl inwards; no finger should extend away from the handle of the cup. Drinking tea from the saucer was once acceptable as a strategy for cooling it but is now almost universally considered a breach of etiquette.

Tea is not only the name of the beverage, but of a late afternoon light meal. Tea Rooms were once very popular in the UK and some still exist. Tea biscuits are what Americans might call cookies or crackers, served with tea on social occasions in Britain as a essential component of British hospitality. Dainty sandwiches were also typical fare, particularly such delicacies as cucumber and watercress sandwiches. In modern Britain, where often all adult members of families are employed, the teapot has often been replaced by the individual teabag, surely a modern sacrilege to the noble legacy of tea drinking in Britain. It does make one ponder about this notion of progress and if what is defined as progress and power in economic and military matters contains the appropriate criteria to evaluate what should represent progress in the culture.

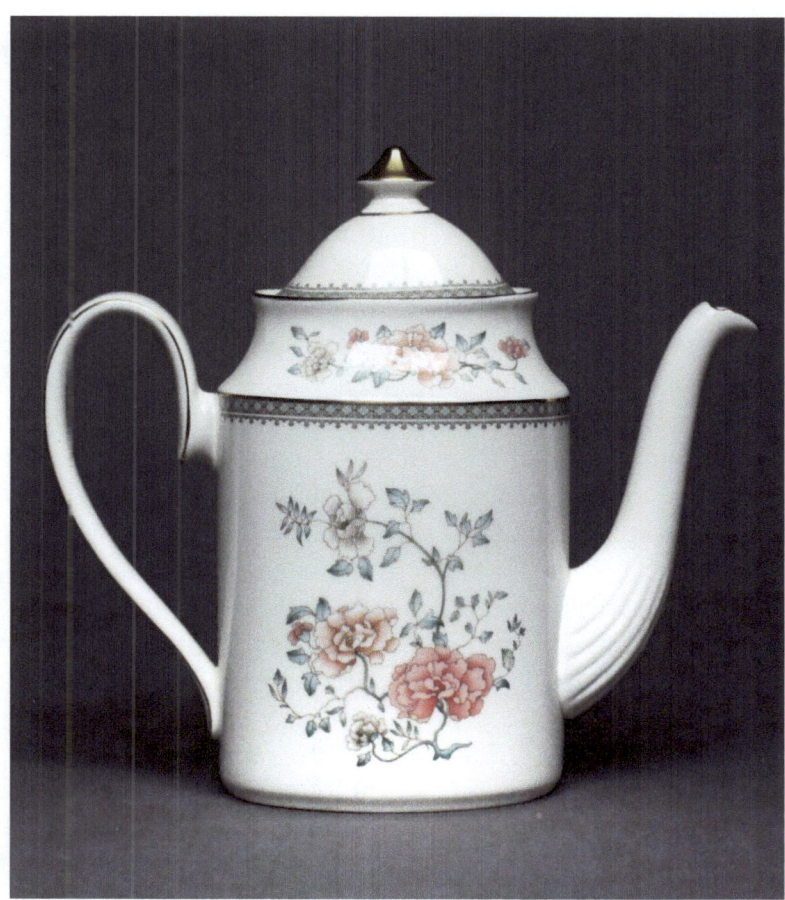

Roya Doulton, Minton
Jasmine Pattern Teapot, c. 1977
Collection of Judy & Richard Jacobs

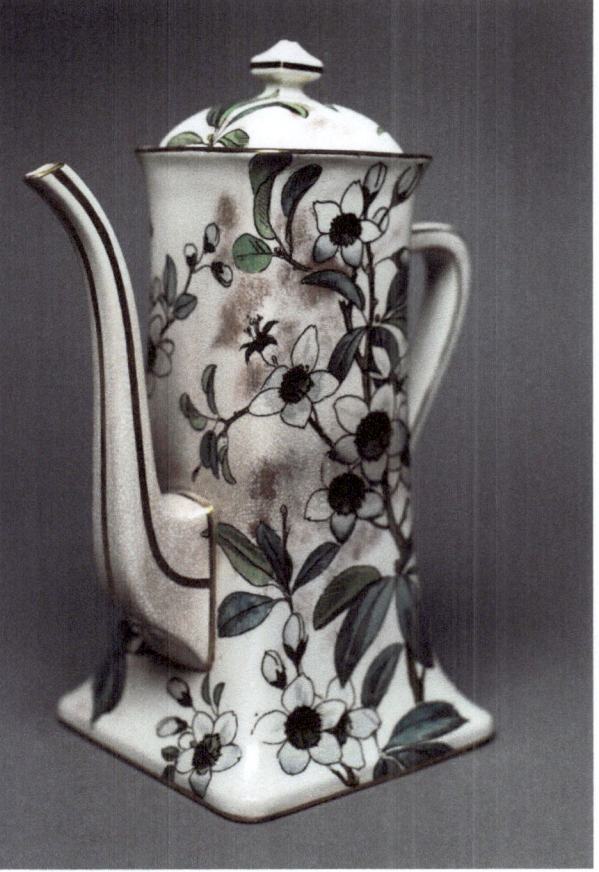

Royal Doulton
Floral Coffee Pot, 1879
Collection of Judy & Richard Jacobs

The Domestic Interior: The Heartland of the British Arts and Crafts Movement

By Dr. Richard Jacobs
California Collector of Ceramics

There was something considered almost sacred about the rights of British people within the private space of their homes. This was in accord with the political ideals of British democratic thought. The common laws of England supported the belief that indeed a man's home was his castle. In rather recent times, after a long struggle, these same rights have been extended as well to women. All notions about the home and indeed the composition and relative rights of family members show the same dynamic shifts of an evolving history.

In Britain during the 19th century there was certainly great contrast between the lordly manor houses of the aristocracy and the thatched cottages of the rural peasants or the cramped hovels of the urban working class. These same contrasts shaped the vastly different character of family life and household conditions at these sites. But all shared this egalitarian spirit regarding their rights within their own domiciles that made each person's home also his private refuge.

It should be noted that the typical or traditional organizational features of British and American families were quite different in many profound respects. In British upper class families, young boys were most often sent away at an early age to boarding schools to live and attend school and came home at holidays and for other special occasions. In the same families, where infants and young girls remained at home, nannies and tutors were employed to care for them and attend to their daily needs. British family life was sectioned into separated spaces within the home and in the differing activities of the men, women and children of the family. This included most meals where children were fed separately and did not attend the more formal dining events of their parents and guests. There were also rooms of the house where male privilege made them mostly off limits for women, including the study, library, and billiard room. After sharing the dining room meal, women were expected to withdraw to the sitting or drawing room and leave the men to their own company. While the downstairs kitchen was entirely populated by women, they were most often employees of their superiors upstairs. Children were housed in the nursery. Everyone had a proper locale within the home and a host of role expectations according to age and gender. Upper class American families might attempt to emulate some of these domestic conventions of their British cousins but clearly the model was of British origin. The domestic order of the home and family among the lower classes and those mired in poverty will not be examined here. The best source for that discussion might well be the novels of Charles Dickens.

William Morris had a profoundly different vision from the description above of what a society should be like and most definitely that included what a home should be like. For Morris, the home was not only the rightful sanctuary of every person regardless of rank and wealth, the home was also meant to be the treasure house of beautifully crafted things. Beauty for him was not in the ostentatious and excessive display of expensive artifacts that advertised

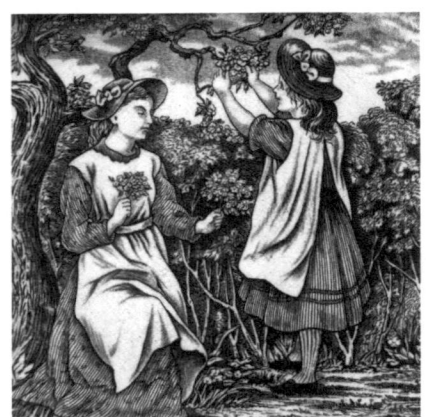

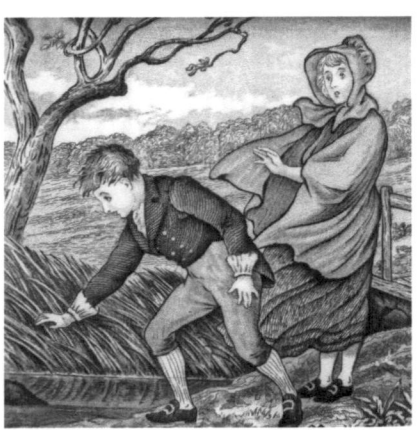

Josiah Wedgwood & Sons *Tile* (top)
Josiah Wedgwood & Co. *Tile*
Collection of Norman Karlson

the great wealth of the owner. For Morris it was the devoted and disciplined work of craftspeople that provided the handcrafted objects that formed and framed the functions and appearances of the home. This vision was not only aesthetic but also normative in that it came from a comprehensive belief that all citizens were entitled to this enhanced and enriched life and the evidence of this exalted existence was to be located in their homes.

We can best understand the importance of the domestic interior to William Morris and the British Arts and Crafts Movement by directly reading his own words and thoughts on the matter. The following are quotes taken from his writings:

"For ... everything made by man's hands has a form, which must be either beautiful or ugly; beautiful if it is in accord with Nature, and help her; ugly if it is discordant with Nature, and thwarts her; it cannot be indifferent...Now it is one of the chief uses of decoration, the chief part of its alliance with nature, that it has to sharpen our dulled senses in the matter: for this end are those wonders of intricate patterns interwoven, those strange forms invented, which men have so long delighted in: forms and intricacies that do not necessarily imitate nature, but in which the hand of the craftsman is guided to work in the way she does, till the web, the cup, or the knife, look as natural, nay as lovely, as the green field, the river bank, or the mountain flint."

"To give people pleasure in the things they must perforce *use*, that is one great office of decoration; to give people pleasure in the things they must perforce *make*, that is the other use of it."

"These arts ... are the sweeteners of human labor, both to the handicraftsman, whose life is spent in working in them, and to people in general, who are influenced by the sight of them at every turn of the day's work: they make our toil happy, our rest fruitful."

"... nothing can be a work of art which is not useful; that is to say, which does not minister to the body when well under command of the mind, or which does not amuse, soothe, or elevate the mind in a healthy state. What tons upon tons of unutterable rubbish pretending to be works of art in some degree would this maxim clear out of our London houses, if it were understood and acted upon!...as a rule all the decoration (so called)...is there for the sake of show, not because anybody likes it. I repeat, this stupidity goes through all classes of society: the silk curtains in my Lord's drawing-room are no more a matter of art to him than the powder in his footman's hair; the kitchen in a country farmhouse is most commonly a pleasant and homelike place, the parlor dreary and useless. I do not want art for a few, any more than education for a few, or freedom for a few."

"*Have nothing in your houses which you do not know to be useful or believe to be beautiful.*"

WORLDWIDE INFLUENCE: THE ROLE OF BRITISH CERAMICS IN THE ARTS & CRAFTS MOVEMENT

By Dr. Richard Jacobs
California Collector of Ceramics

This Arts and Crafts Movement began in the mid-Victorian era and continued to some degree in Britain through the first two decades of the 20th century. By the time of World War I and its horrific impact on Britain, the decline of this movement was evident and other aesthetic trends clearly came to the fore. William Morris was the leader of the Arts and Crafts Movement in Britain. His leadership was centered on reviving or retaining handicraft traditions in the face of increasing mechanization. These efforts were at the heart of the British Arts and Crafts Movement. The art critic and social reformer, John Ruskin, was a great influence on Morris and inspired and informed the direction he took. Ruskin asserted that mechanization was dehumanizing, and impacted not only the quality of life but degraded craftsmanship itself. He also championed the Gothic style derived from the medieval period as superior to all others because it was the least mechanistic. Morris developed strong theories of his own which soon made him the leader in this movement. The Arts and Crafts Movement influenced many fields, including architecture, handicrafts and both the fine and applied arts. This school of thought was very inclusive in that it endorsed everyday objects such as flower vases, tableware, and furniture, all located in the domestic interior of the home, as having the same corresponding aesthetic importance as painting and sculpture. This kind of thinking encouraged the market for aesthetic objects and promoted a number of ceramic manufacturers to set up special departments to design and produce art pottery.

William Morris was a man of vast talents, a gifted writer, poet, as well as a social idealist and political activist. He was someone who had a wide span of interests and abilities that continued to expand as he became a designer and craftsman. His influence extended to innovations in ceramics by pottery manufacturers such as Doulton & Co., and ceramic artists such the Martin brothers and his good friend, William De Morgan. Given the ongoing industrialization of Britain at the time, today we might consider Morris's goals to revert back to the medieval guilds as a craft-based model that would allow the individual artisan to remain involved in all aspects of production a bit naive if not impractical. His dreams were not limited to the artisan, and his egalitarian ideals for a society where all enjoyed the fruits of human labor in a communal society were also most worthy, even if they too suffered by not being grounded in the harsh realities of the day. To his credit, he did live by his ideals, mastering a range of different crafts, creating a craft-cooperative to build and decorate his new home, Red House, and establishing a business that employed many craftspeople. His firm received many commissions that represented a wide diversity of crafts, including the design and creation of furniture, textiles, wallpaper, stained glass windows, tiles and the design and publication of books. Morris joined with others of shared ideals to tirelessly promote his aesthetic and social causes. It was said at the time of his death that he simply died of complete exhaustion; just being William Morris had been sufficient to bring about his demise.

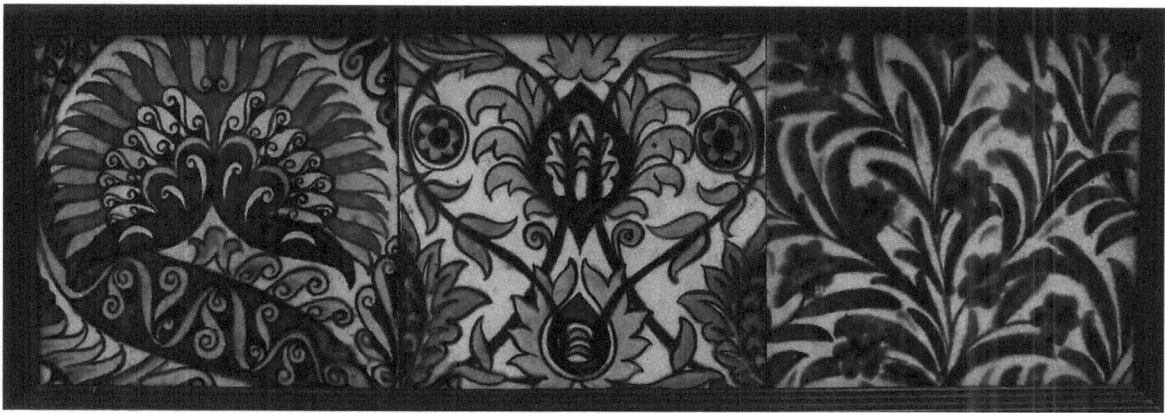

William DeMorgan
Framed Tiles, c. 1880
Collection of Norman Karlson

William De Morgan was intimately involved with Morris and the Arts & Crafts Movement in Britain and was a master ceramic artist. De Morgan was also influenced by Turkish and Persian designs and he sought to rediscover the lusters of the 14th and 15th centuries in those ceramic traditions. Much of his work was based on the use of copper and silver; the colors so produced included pink, yellow and grey luster decoration. He applied these techniques and effects to both his tiles and his vessels. He also explored designs that portrayed animals, fantastic beasts, ornate foliage and ships. De Morgan received varied commissions including tiles, panels, and plates for luxury liners and the homes of distinguished patrons. His work often projected vivid and brilliant colors, blue, turquoise, green and clear red, often involved in flowing and intricate designs. Much of this decoration shared an affinity with the wallpaper and fabric designs of William Morris.

In a sense, William De Morgan signaled the arrival of the independent artist-potter, working outside the paternal security of the large industrial ceramic firm. It is an interesting facet of his work that de Morgan did not throw his own pots, thinking that a lesser workman could accomplish that feat or he could have recourse to using industrial blanks. So he did not achieve the complete transformation to Morris's ideal of the artisan to handcraft the complete artifact, nor did he make the entire transition to the artist-potter as the sole maker. This was counter to the notion, once prevalent in America and widely believed in Britain, that the more significant and important task in pottery was in the throwing of the clay form itself, largely restricted to men in the industrial potteries, while it was women's work to do the decoration. This notion was compounded in America by a far more puritanical notion common in the Arts & Crafts Movement here that decoration itself was an unwelcome and excessive addition to the elegance of the form and the matte finish of a single glaze. Simplicity and economy in decoration and tenor of expression was a central tenet of American Arts & Crafts pottery. This was not the case generally in Britain. Obviously De Morgan in his unique manner agreed with a most elaborate, if not exotic, approach.

Henry Doulton applied the aesthetic principles of art and craft theories by setting up a separate studio at his factory specifically for ceramic design and decoration. Towards the end of the 19th century, over three hundred people were employed in this art studio department. In 1872 earthenware was introduced in the studio and further experiments led to the making of 'faience,' a term covering earthenware with relief molding decorated with colored glazes. Other ceramic firms also established these 'art pottery studios' autonomous from their larger industrial operations. This practice greatly encouraged the trend toward the artist-potter. There still might be separate functions at these firms for the thrower and decorator, but both were committed to individual expression within the aesthetic confines of an overall 'house' style.

There are many ironies embedded in the Arts & Crafts Movement in Britain. The progressive social and political ideology and idealism inherent in the beliefs of Morris and his friends that their craft should be made available to all was obstructed by the economic reality that such time consuming handcrafted work could only be afforded by the very rich. The reformist fervor associated with the movement faded, caused in part by the demise of Morris prior to the turn of the century and to the changing world around them. Most of the British potters associated with this movement were focused on the glaze and decorative elements of pottery, while in France, America and elsewhere studio potters were emerging who functioned as independent artists. The eventual demise of any artistic movement does not necessarily signify inherent inadequacies or profound failure. The historical and cultural context of changing times often renders harsh verdicts that make whatever went before it appear obsolete despite its worthy content and cultural benefit. The overall virtues of the movement included respect for the natural qualities of the crafted medium, devotion to the handcrafted artifact and the ability of the single artisan to fashion it whole, and a moral commitment to ameliorate and enrich the lives of those ordinary citizens that might obtain such work. All are still part of a respected aesthetic that is still prized and continues to influence arts and crafts today.

Minton & Co. *Tile*
Collection of
Norman Karlson

MAW & Co. *Tile*
Collection of
Norman Karlson

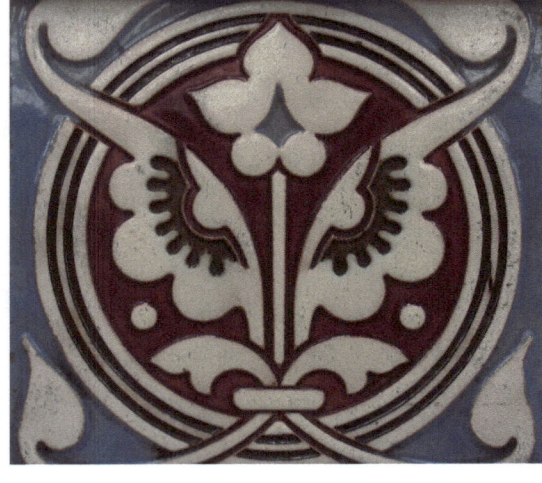
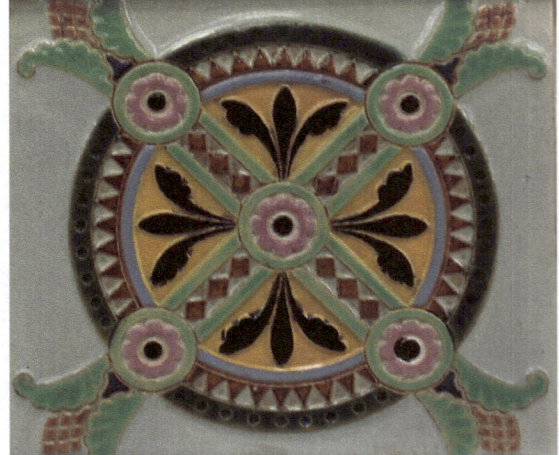

THE BRITISH STUDIO ART POTTER: THE STRUGGLE BETWEEN TRADITION AND MODERNISM IN THE 20TH CENTURY

By Dr. Richard Jacobs
California Collector of Ceramics

The emergence of the independent studio potter coincided with the advent of modernism in the late 19th and early 20th century. These studio potters mixed their own clay, developed their own glazes, fired their own kilns and controlled every aspect of their craft. Many of the earlier efforts remained devoted to domestic wares, reinforcing the British tendency toward a practical utility and common sense in all things. The notable pioneers of the British Studio Art Movement were not humble in their origins or modest in their aspirations. Bernard Leach, Michael Cardew, and William Staite Murray were intellectuals, mostly from middle or upper class backgrounds, well educated, products of privilege. These studio art potters were traditionalists in their devotion to the vessel, but unlike the prior Arts & Crafts Movement associated with William Morris, they found their inspiration in early Chinese stoneware and, to a lesser degree, in British slipware.

Leach and others celebrated what they termed 'the ethical pot.' This template contained the virtues and 'pure' traditions of Chinese Sung pottery that included truth to materials and a reverence for tradition and utility. The purpose of their daily use in the ordinary lives of ordinary people carried a presumed moral superiority according to this view. Murray somewhat deviated from this view, defending the 'fine art pot' as a work of art. Leach assumed almost a prophet status, eager to return from numerous visits and stays in Japan to introduce to Western potters the glory and mystery of Eastern ceramics. He also wrote books that became classics still read and revered today, his first manifesto being "A Potter's Outlook," followed later by "A Potter's Book." Yet more books came toward the end of his life. Michael Cardew was the first Western apprentice of Leach; others soon

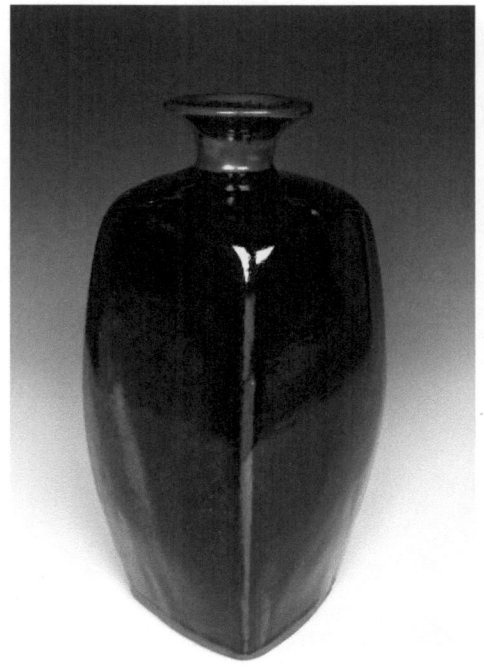
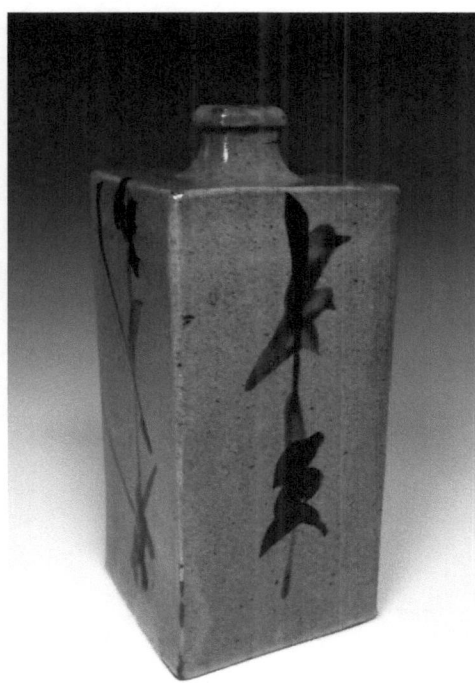

Bernard Leach (1887-1979)
Bottle, Early 20th Century
Collection of Julianne &
David Armstrong

Shoji Hamada (1894-1978)
Square Bottle,
Early 20th Century
Collection of Sharon &
Paul Dauer

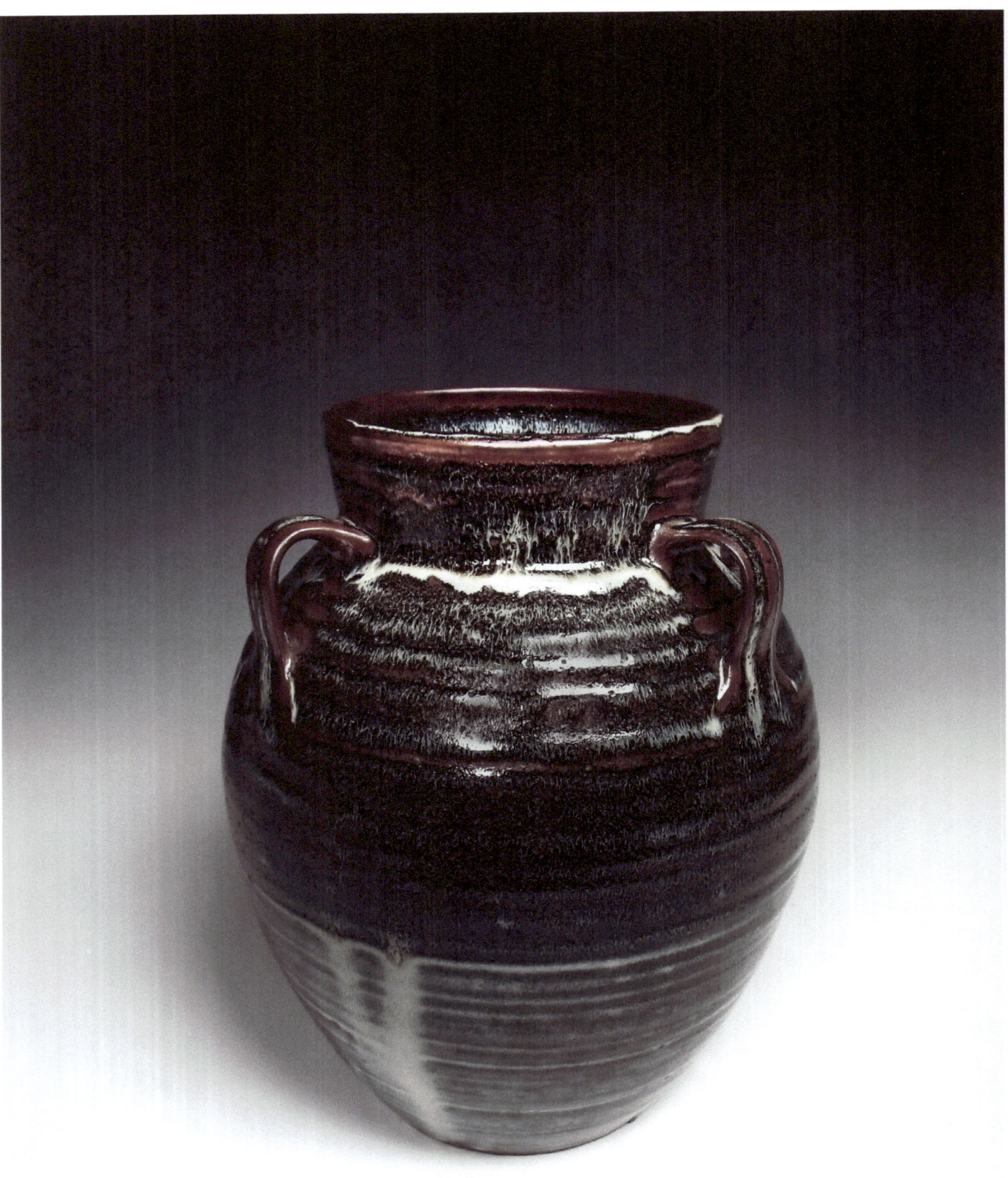

joined them. It is important to note that Leach, Murray and Cardew made a living by their ceramic work, with a growing group of collectors purchasing their wares. They took in young apprentices who developed into leading art potters of the next generation. As with the crafts that came out of the workshops of William Morris in the previous century, the prices charged by these art potters were not affordable to the average Briton.

Leach did not limit his efforts in influencing the aesthetic direction of ceramics to Japan and Britain. His travels and lectures included touring the United States with Shoji Hamada, an outstanding potter in his own right, and Soetsu Yangi, the leader of the Mingei Movement in Japan. As his influence continued into mid-twentieth century, Leach was perceived by some as a restraining and rigidly conservative voice in British ceramics. After World War II, this backlash became more vehement and other quite different viewpoints and work became prominent. Even someone like Michael Cardew, once his apprentice, remarked that Leach was a 'perfectly preserved Edwardian'. Today we can provide a proper and balanced tribute that fully concedes that Leach provided potters with an informed confidence and infused pottery with spirituality and intelligence that had not been present before.

In the post-war period of the 1950s and the 1960s, many potters attempted to have the best of two worlds, producing functional and traditional pottery termed domestic ware, quite popular at the time and providing a steady income, while also attempting one-of-a-kind 'art' pots that allowed their creative spirits fuller expression. Bernard Leach produced a ceramic dynasty of his own, with his sons David and Michael and grandsons John and Jeremy becoming potters. It was a very good time for ceramics in Britain. Art and craft education was being greatly expanded. Studio pottery attracted a greater audience of potential consumers. This is in unfortunate contrast to the situation today. The functional tradition today in Britain is in crisis. Many ceramics programs at colleges, universities and art schools that once focused on developing potters are either closing down or throwing away their potter's wheels in favor of an integration of ceramics with design, fine art departments or sculpture programs in which clay might be one media among many. The romance of rustic crafts has given way to more urbane and modern notions of aesthetic taste.

Two strands competed during this post-Second World War period for the favor of the makers of ceramics; one was the ideas based on traditional Asian forms that continued to provide tableware that could be traced to Leach, a second consisted of interpretations based on ideas emanating from the Continent and centered around concepts of modernism in the arts. These two competing strands each had their own advocates, often offering very different viewpoints concerning the future of ceramic ware: either followed the legacy of creating domestic tableware as an honorable craft or the contrasting perspective of clay as the expressive media of the creative

Left:
Michael Cardew, (1901-1983)
Jug, Early 20th Century
Collection of Scripps College, Claremont, CA, Gift of Mr. & Mrs. Fred Marer

artist. Others attempted an aesthetic compromise in viewing the positive possibilities of both craft and art in their ceramic artifacts. Sometimes this effort at mastery of the media and a unique creative expression happened regardless of their own self-declared definition as to which school of making they belonged to and whether the intended site of their work was to be the home or art gallery. For some of them who favored the domestic site, the drawing room was a preferred site for their work rather than the scullery or dining room.

Three ceramic artists who achieved such a synthesis in post-war Britain were Lucie Rie, Hans Coper and Ruth Duckworth. The influence of modern notions of design on the European continent was imported into Britain by the arrival of these refugees from the rise of Hitler and Nazism in Germany during the 1930s. Rie brought with her the principles of Bauhaus design that emphasized an abstracted simplicity. She gave her ceramics a rich and experimental use of color and texture. She established her status and reputation as a major ceramic artist in Britain and spent the remainder of her life in London. Her pottery emphasized form, rather than decoration, and glaze and body color that displayed a range of dry, gritty, textured surfaces. She became a firm friend of Leach, took his advice and instruction on her pottery, and maintained a high regard for his work. Rie has great influence as a potter and teacher. She attained international acclaim, making pots well into her late 80s.

For some years after the war, Rie worked in partnership with Hans Coper, another refugee from Germany. He saw himself primarily as a sculptor and developed an individual style quite different from that of Rie. Coper achieved a synthesis of both worlds in that he was influenced by ancient Egyptian and Cycladic pots and achieved those forms following the highest traditions of craft, while exhibiting a high degree of personal expression in his ceramic work. Coper and Rie worked in the same workshop for years, and exhibited together, truly complementing each other in their work. They were both disciplined perfectionists, two great European potters that became firmly anchored in British cultural life, contributing through their unique gifts a vision and inspiration that enriched the early post-war period in Britain.

Duckworth was of a different ceramic stripe than Rie and Coper. She was a sculptural potter, sacrificing an elegance of form and surface beauty for a more strident and unsymmetrical expression. She moved a greater distance than either Rie or Coper toward sculptural forms that were distinctly modern in result and effect. Her aesthetic motivation was inspired by attempting to attain an organic abstraction that went beyond simple geometry with a free flowing biomorphism that provided others at the time with a liberating example of possibilities. Duckworth left Britain for America and became an important presence in the ceramic art world in this country.

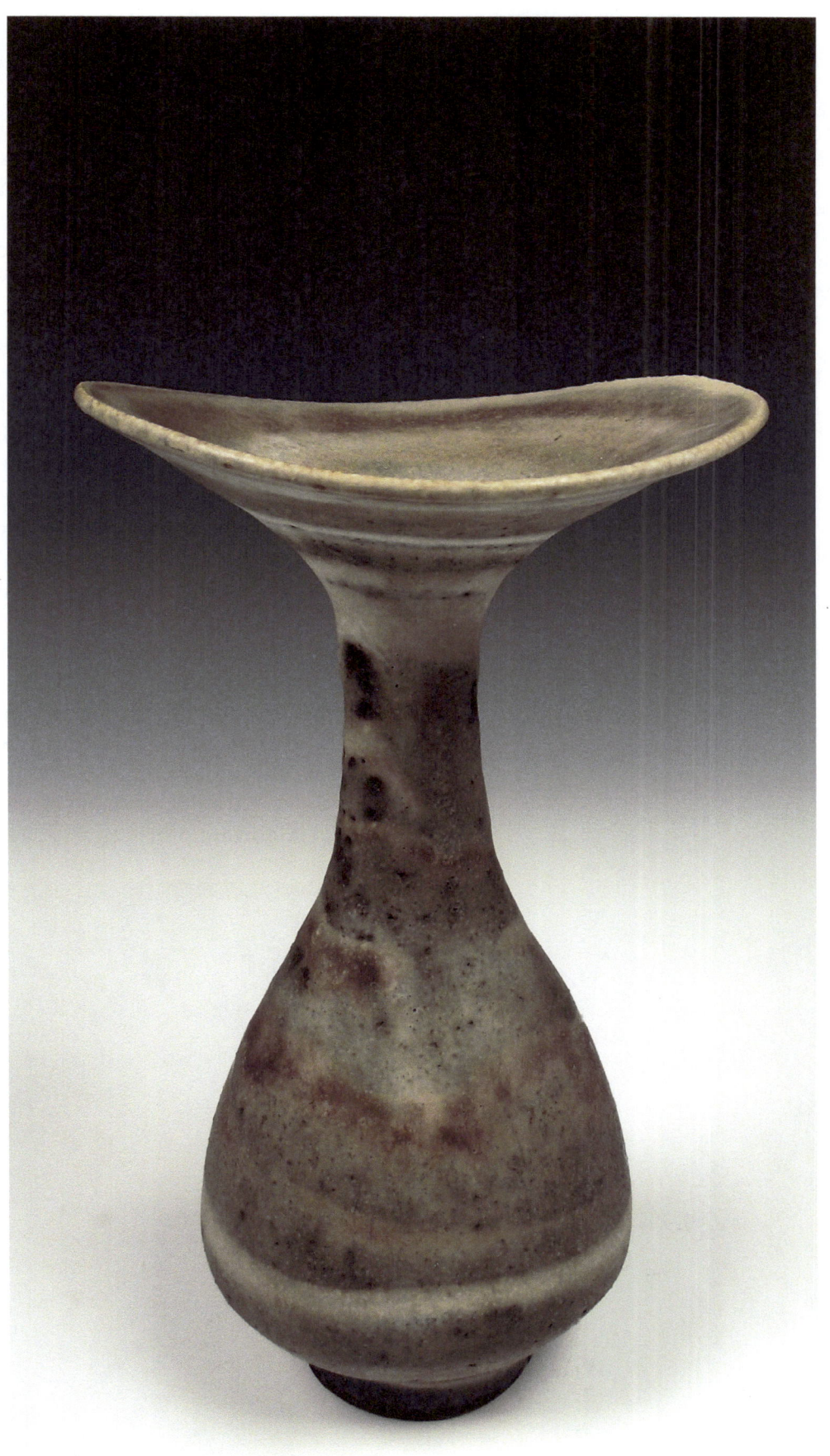

Lucie Rie (1902-1995)
Bottle, 20th Century
Collection of Hannah &
Russel Kully

What is the case for tradition for the contemporary potter? Is it a lost cause? One place to examine this question is to visit the Craft Potters Association (CPA) of Great Britain, a national body representing ceramic artists in the UK. It is the organizing agent of professional potters, providing their own gallery for the exhibit of member's work in London, as well as holding exhibitions throughout Britain. This invitational body includes senior potters identified as Fellows, as well as over 200 professional and 500 associate members. The CPA publishes the Ceramic Review, a highly regarded journal on contemporary ceramics. One of the most important annual events that CPA sponsors is Ceramic Art London, a major international fair and educational program, held at the Royal College of Art in London. They are the major catalyst in Britain for the public display of British ceramics and that exposure to the public that seeks to find new audiences. It is evident from attending their exhibits that there remains a predominance of members that still work within the creative arena of pottery as vessel and container.

Mark Hewitt is an eloquent spokesperson for the values and virtues of tradition for the potter. Born in Britain, Hewitt was the son and grandson of managers of the Spode Ceramic Works in Stoke-on-Trent, the heart of the potteries in the midlands of Britain. He was a student of Michael Cardew, left Britain for America as a young man, and settled in North Carolina where vernacular ceramic traditions spanned generations of potters. He remains an active and important potter to this day.

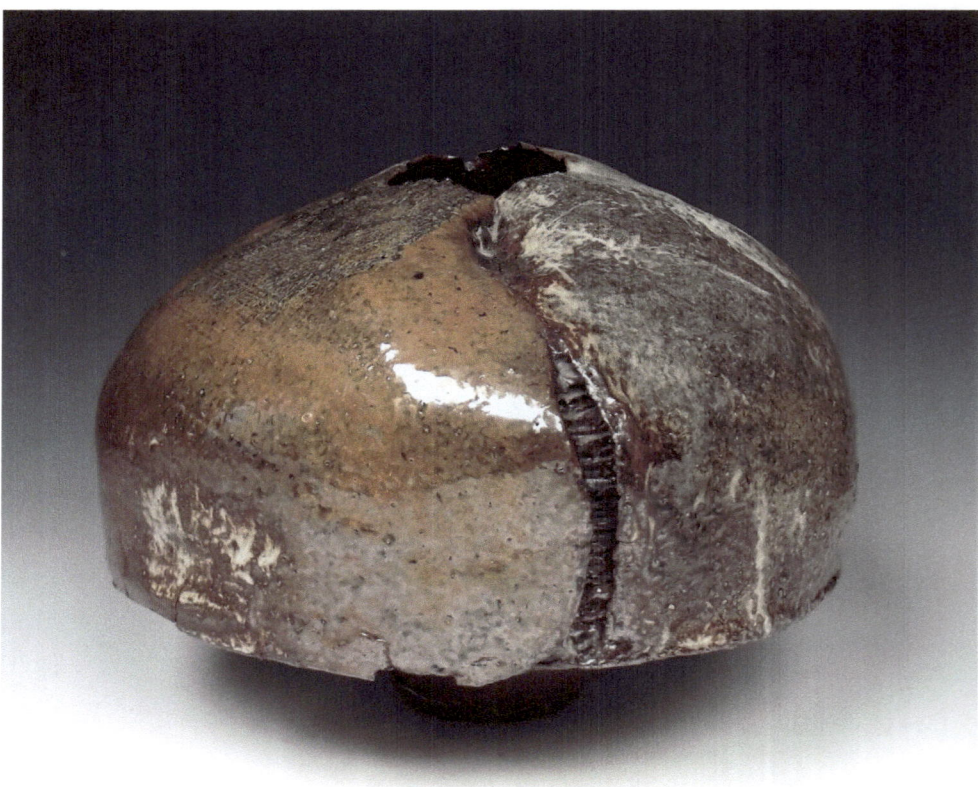

Ruth Duckworth (1919-2009)
Vessel, 20th Century
Collection of Kent Tool

This is what Hewitt had to say in favor of tradition in the book that he co-authored, "The Potter's Eye":

"Tradition is good, tradition is beautiful, tradition is valuable. To say so is unconventional and a little dangerous, for as T.S. Eliot wrote in his essay *Tradition and the Individual Talent*, 'Seldom, perhaps, does the word appear except in a phrase of censure.' Indeed, tradition is often perceived as a hindrance to individualism and artistic originality. But I agree with Eliot that the opposite is true. In his words, 'No poet, no artist of any art, has his complete meaning alone. His significance, his appreciation is the appreciation of his relation to the dead poets and artists.' Thus we must look to the past, to the very roots of our art, to guide us toward new forms of self-expression. Potters and ceramic artists use ceramic history and particular traditions to inform their work and those traditions inspire rather than discourage innovation."

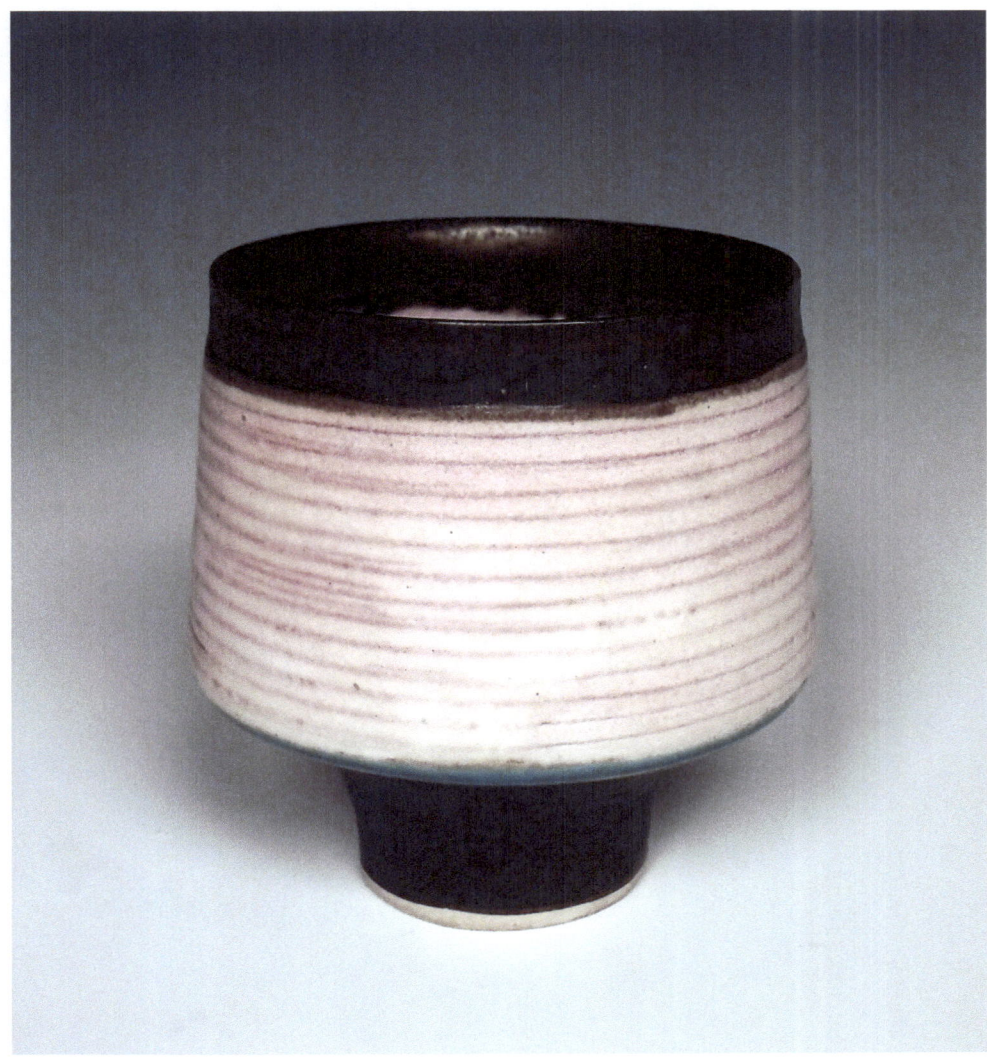

Lucie Rie
Footed Bowl, 20th Century
Collection of Sharon &
Paul Dauer

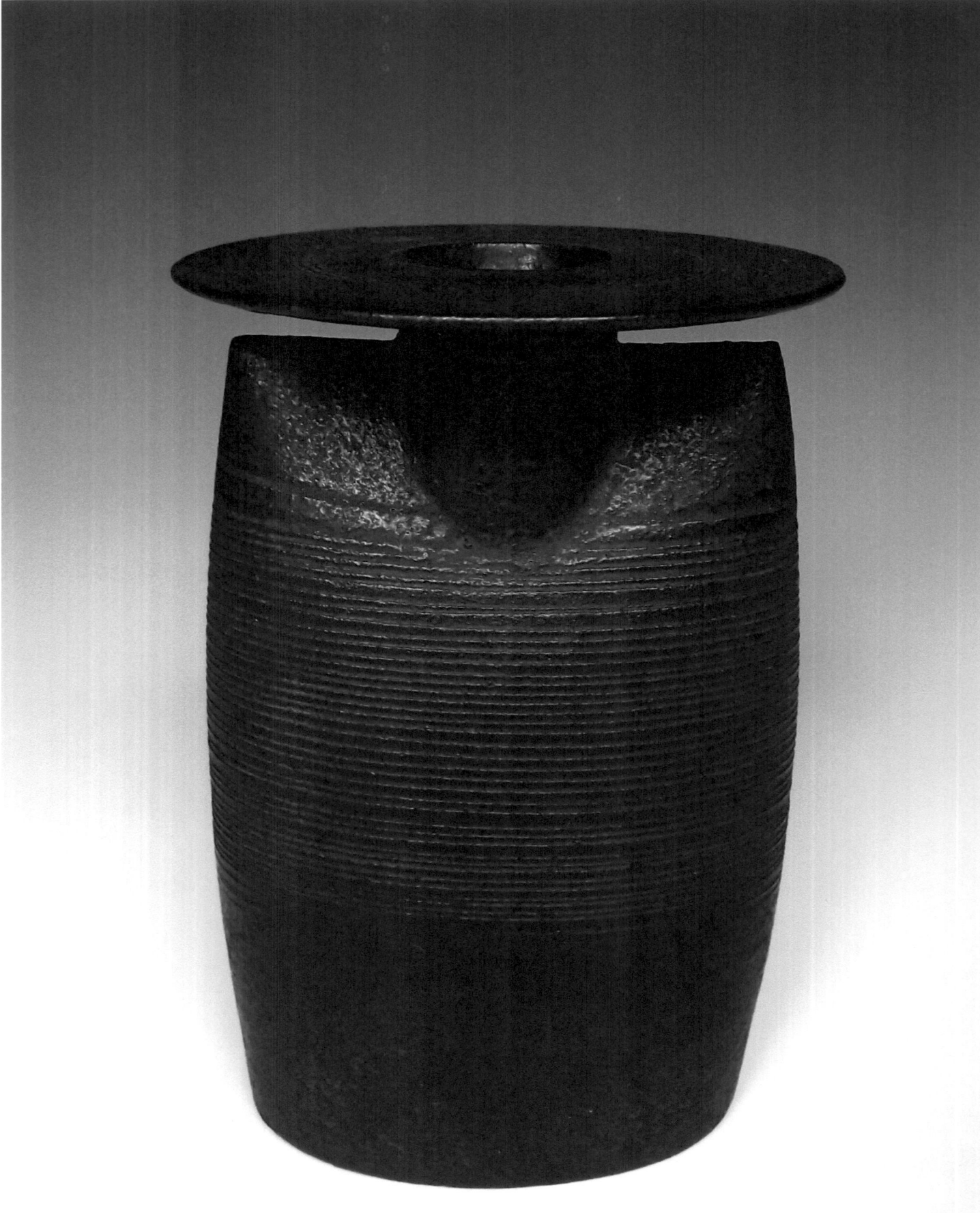

THE CULTURAL IMPACT OF MODERNISM: LOSS OF INNOCENCE OR THE TRIUMPH OF SOPHISTICATION?

By Dr. Richard Jacobs
California Collector of Ceramics

We know that we cannot affix a single time or date for the beginning of an age or the end of one. Human civilization and history does not work that way. Whatever scholars and authorities might register as calendar approximations for the emergence of modernism, are not all cultures modern in the moment of their immediate existence when compared to their past? What is the difference between being contemporary in that sense and what we would call modern today? Are there novel characteristics of human ways of perceiving and living in the world that occurred during the late 19th and the length of much of the 20th century that were so profound in their impact that the world has never been the same since?

People in the West tend to calibrate what is modern according to the advance of technology and material progress. But here we are examining what it means to call human culture and behavior modern. We locate its nature by examining our ways of being alive and conscious in the world and how we make sense of that world. These novel literary and visual vocabularies of modernism were unique forms of expression when they made their appearance in the arts and literature. On these occasions, some segments of British society celebrated manifestations of their arrival and appearances and some were deeply shocked by it. After establishing that greater cultural context, we can then place ceramics within this time, looking for those same characteristics in clay artifacts that mark and reflect this radical and revolutionary period of innovation and experimentation that we call modernism.

Virginia Woolf, the British novelist, famously declared, "… on or about December 10 1910, human character changed." She was perhaps being facetious, but her point was that although the Edwardian age was over, the conventional habits of that staid and somewhat stagnant period lingered on afterwards in its literature and elsewhere in the culture. Modernism was quite subversive, railing against convention in every aspect of society and culture. Is beingwell situated and respectable the normal goal of individuals in a stable and civilized society? Would not conformity be a small price to pay for such a society? In Britain it was more the circumstances of your birth within a class that determined both your status and your future. But modernism called for social heresy, transgressing rules that had governed traditional art and culture for centuries. Modernists in the arts were often, at least at first, considered cultural outlaws, even dangerous in their impact and consequences.

We must give proper credit to three giants of Western intellectual thought for being the remote patrons of this ongoing upheaval. None of them were poets or artists, but they changed forever the playing field for all artists, including ceramic artists. All three were controversial and in some sense, still are the source of passionate dispute. The first would be Charles Darwin, the scientist who proposed that human beings were a species that evolved

Left:
Hans Coper, (1920-1981)
Vessel, 20th Century
Collection of Sharon &
Paul Dauer

within a family of similar animals by natural selection. This turned religious beliefs upside down at the time and implied a fall from grace from our former status as creatures of a privileged creation. The second visionary was Karl Marx, who lived in Britain during the 19th century, observed the desperate plight of industrial workers, and proposed theories that called for the overthrow of a privileged class that owned the means of production. Notions of what constitutes social and economic justice were constant sources of friction during this time and helped sponsor the labor movement in Britain. The third intellectual rebel was Sigmund Freud, who invented, in a sense, psychoanalysis as a methodology of treating emotional disturbances and further proposed, among other things, that human sexuality, and the suppression of that sexuality by social regulation, was the deep seated instigator of much of our individual and collective problems.

The devastating losses suffered by Britain in World War I, and with it the loss of innocence caused by the slaughter of a whole generation of young British men, resulted in the realization that things could never be the same as they were before. The collective innocence associated with the very notion of a continued and infinite progress in human affairs and civilization was crushed and never quite recovered. Those same intellectual forces and the war also sponsored pessimism about the human condition, a weary if not cynical view of the limitations of our species that was often displayed in the arts by satirical and critical attacks on conventional ways of thinking – that many moderns thought had gotten them into such a mess in the first place. Business as usual was out – and that included ceramics as well.

All this turmoil was counter balanced by the liberating energy of those artists who threw off the habits of the discredited past and took the opportunities to revise our notions of what constitutes expression and creativity in all the various media. It was a time of experimentation and innovation in all the arts, rules were meant to be broken, and nothing was fixed anymore. There was no longer a general consensus or agreement about what would be the accepted givens that could still be trusted to endure. And most of all, there was no central authority reinforced by status or power that could suppress the erupting genius of an untrammeled creative spirit. Hitler tried to do that very thing, labeling modern art in the 1930's in Germany as decadent art, removing work from museums, forcing artists to flee, and others, who unfortunately did not escape, to withdraw from sight in order to survive. But Britain emerged victorious in that war and modernism also endured and shared that victory.

It is at this juncture that Lucie Rie, Hans Coper, and Ruth Duckworth arrived in England, bringing with them a sophisticated and inclusive view of the currents and contributions of a dynamic European modernism that was being suppressed on the continent by fascism at the time. The possible range of expression in modernism was as extensive as the individual imagination. It was never a single school or movement. This 'shock of the new' continues today. Perhaps the most important attribute of those who experience and engage the ceramic arts requires at first a forgiving tolerance, a willingness to witness forms of expression not evident in those elegant teacups of 19th century Britain. This open attitude allows a self-imposed innocence on the part of the observer of modern ceramics that can lead to a more enduring and inclusive insight that one does not have to reject or nullify the virtues of the teacup in order to embrace the more expressive or abstracted artifacts of the modern age. Thus we can remain innocent in our immediate joy in engaging art, while finding our own approximation of a wise sophistication that celebrates multiple ways of living and experiencing the world for both maker and observer.

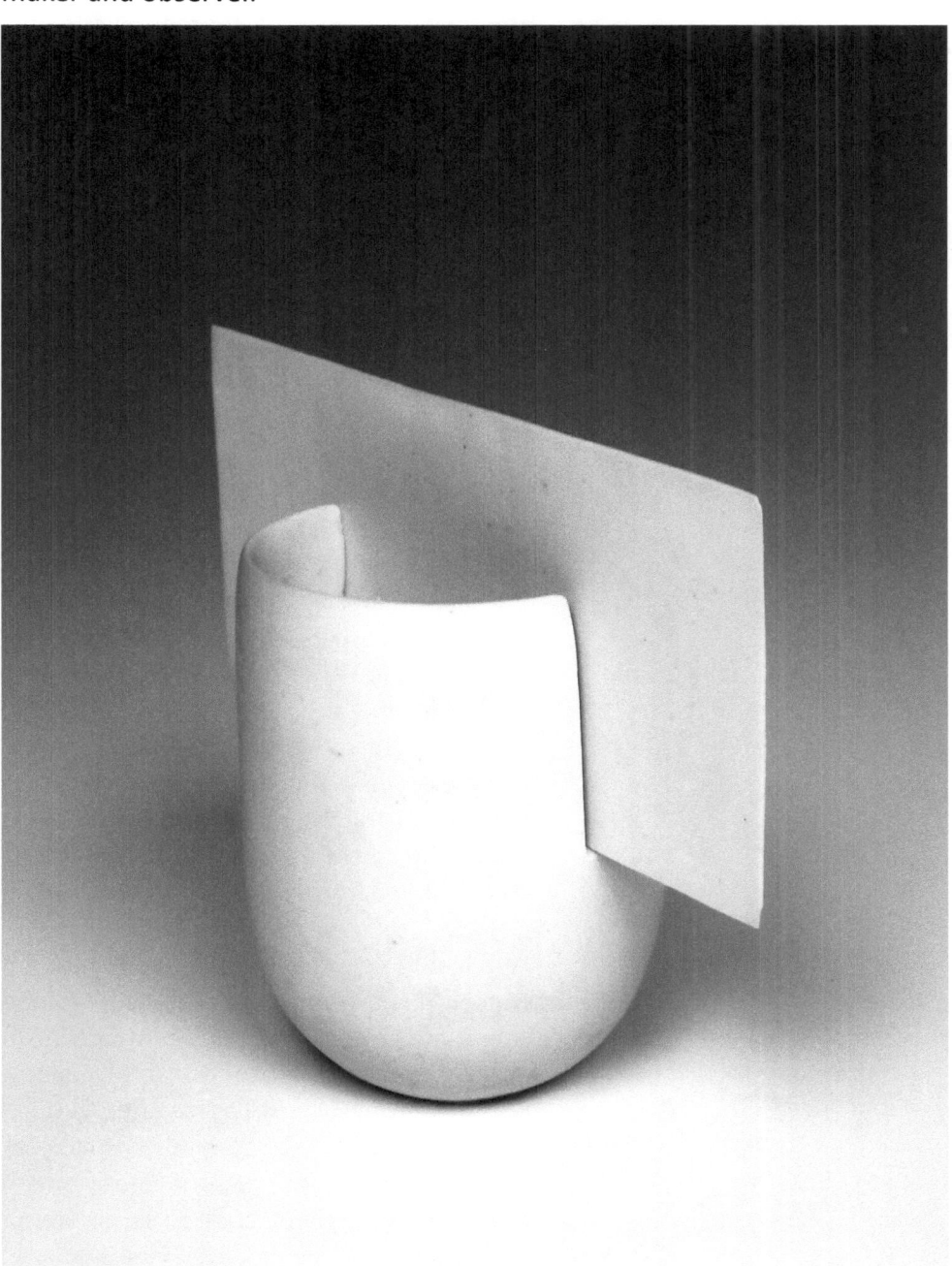

Ruth Duckworth
Blade Sculpture,
20th Century
Collection of Marcella Ruble

POSTMODERN BRITISH CERAMICS: CAN NEW MEANINGS AND OBJECTS BE CREATED OUT OF THE MEANINGS AND OBJECTS OF THE PAST?

By Dr. Richard Jacobs
California Collector of Ceramics

Why would you appropriate ideas from modernism when you are trying to go beyond it? Even the term of postmodernism is composed of a partial tribute to what some are trying to escape or overcome. Is postmodernism more a rejection of modernism than it is a repudiation of those traditions that existed prior to modernism? Is it a surreptitious, even sentimental attempt to retrieve and revive discarded bits and pieces of a past once thought aesthetically obsolete? Postmodern ceramic artists have some of the same attitudes as previous generations of modern artists. This includes a dislike of authority and a lack of reverence for the past that often takes the form of humor or satire, some of it quite harsh in intent and character in regard to their attitude toward their belated acquisitions. Post-modernists might loot the past for ideas and themes as scavengers might sort through dumpsters in urban alleys, delighted with the broken fragments of ceramic history only because they see value in them that has nothing do with their original identity and purpose. It is difficult to judge motives in all cases – are these postmodernists paying a kind of rough tribute to the past or just making fun of it? It might be rather difficult to find a sentimental postmodernist.

Postmodernism is a big tent and houses a wide range of styles, theories, and approaches to art. It can range from a spare minimalism to a highly patterned maximalism. It is essentially eclectic, not necessarily seeking common elements from different periods but rather more ambiguous placement of often-irreconcilable elements in an uncomfortable juxtaposition. The appearance of a postmodern piece can be likened to a visual database of memories from different eras over an extended lifetime. No promise is made that everything will add up or eventually make sense. How can the past be the starting point for something new? The contempt of modernism for decoration was challenged by the postmodern affinity for ornament. These decorative languages contain the visual vocabularies for narration of some sort, not always coherent, but any form of communication can become desirable and valued. There is a rapid-fire intensity and drama in much postmodernism. It has much in common with our electronic age, where we can create instant collages of discreet material sourced from different media with electronic ease. No contemporary experience seems to have a single source or be composed of just one thing. A postmodernist piece seems to have many parents.

Right:
Angela Verdon
Sculpture, 20th Century
Collection of Carolyn &
Sam Black

Applicable to this exhibition hosted by Los Angeles County's American Museum of Ceramic Art, it is worth knowing that Los Angeles was one of the major ceramic sites of postmodernism during the 1960s and 1970s. It is also fitting that the other base of postmodern ceramic activity at this time was Britain. It was in Los Angeles that Peter Voulkos founded with his own work and led by example what has been called the Abstract Expressionist Ceramics Movement. Paul Soldner and Ken Price are two examples of this movement. Soldner created large compositions of sculptural forms often composed of slabs of clay. Price worked in a vivid, primary palette applied

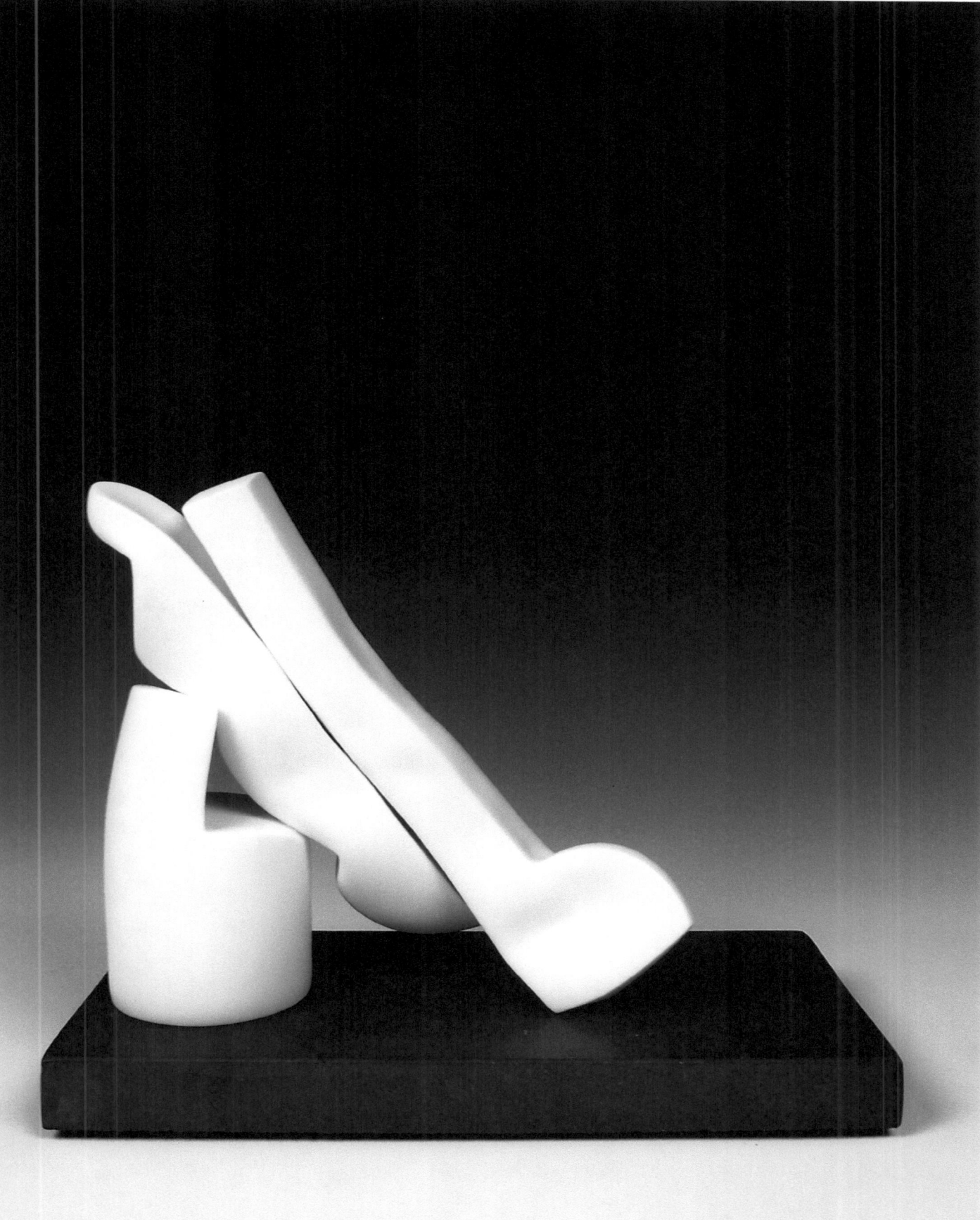

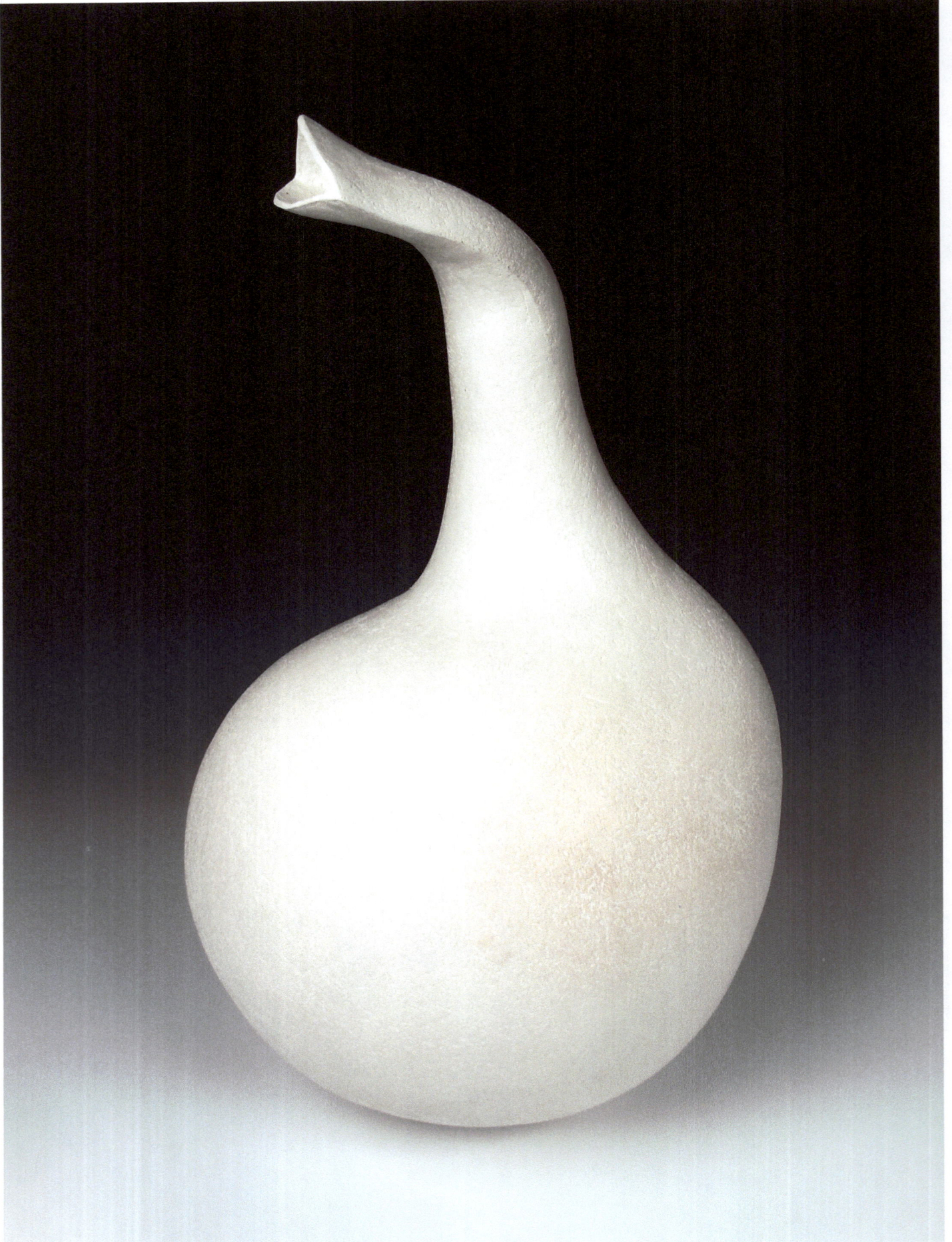

to often highly polished abstract forms, some playful or fanciful takeoffs on more conventional forms of the past.

In this same period in Britain, the Royal College of Arts played an important role in promoting students to free their artistic intuitions and break all rules while doing so. Allison Britton combined use of pattern and decoration in her work with a kind of kinetic surface energy in her slab-built pots. Elizabeth Fritsch flattened her forms and treated them pictorially rather than as fully three-dimensional objects, making full use of surface decoration.

Critics of Postmodernism have not always been kind to this movement. There have been charges of a vulgar emulation of commercial and manufactured commodities that have successfully retained the cheap and common characteristics of the original product. There is a difference between critically mimicking the vulgar and faithfully reproducing it that has sometimes been lost with some post-modernists. Satire cannot exist if it is caught celebrating what it is commenting on. Some have found it difficult to replace the old fashioned affection for the beautiful with many of the postmodern blandishments that appear to favor the ugly, but then beauty and the sublime has been considered traditional adversaries for much of our past aesthetic history. Those who have furthered conceptualism have often offered ideas as excuses or inspiration for their efforts that some see as banal as the subject matter of their work. It is difficult for some to understand how the display of trite and trivial fragments of popular cultures of the past nourishes profundity in the postmodern work that cites it.

Yet we must balance that assessment with the possibilities that the flood of vibrant and fresh post-modern ceramic works in the last few decades of the 20th century have contributed much to the aesthetic richness of our lives. We have a dazzling array of insurgent color, and dense and intricate patterns have been revived that delight the eye. Postmodernist work encourages our own reactions and involvement, and humor and sarcasm can seem to cooperate and operate at the same time and in the same work. It is tolerant and open, arms extended to embrace the common as well as the exotic, the ordinary as well as the extraordinary. Postmodernism rejects a militant and dogmatic stance, often the bane of previous movements, and refuses to be regulated or to regulate others with a single formula. To this extent it very much represents our time and world; a globalization of ceramic effort common to the interaction and interdependence of instant contact between diverse perspectives and cultures that are constantly creating new and complex hybrids of thought and art. Postmodernism has provided the most serious and accepted evidence that ceramics can be considered as art, instead as only craft. Clay has now joined marble, stone, and metal as a valid material for memorable art.

Left:
Betty Blandino
Bottle, 20th Century
Collection of Lynn Myers

CATALOGUE

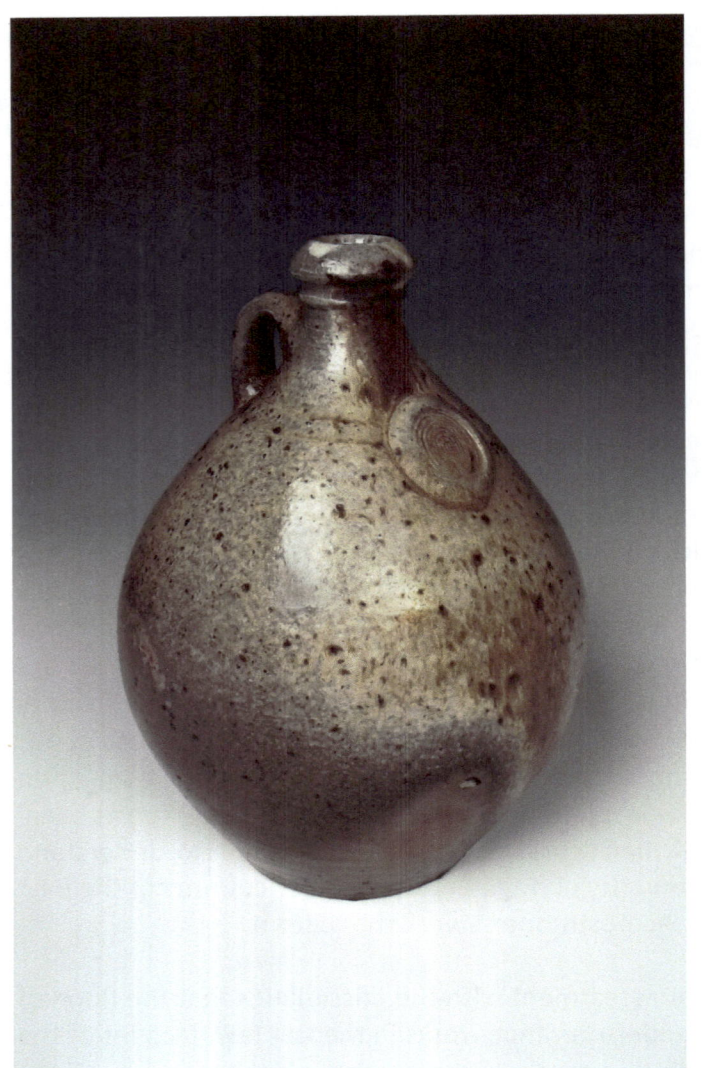

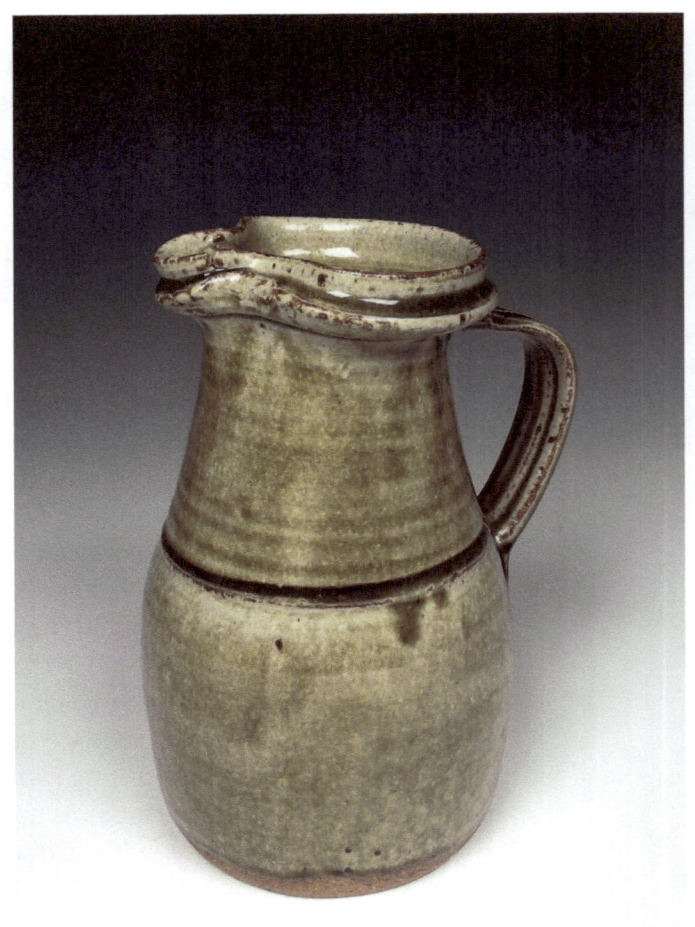

Svend Bayer, (b. 1946)
Jug, 20th Century
Collection of Hannah &
Russel Kully

Richard Batterham, (b. 1936)
Pitcher, 20th Century
AMOCA Permanent Collection,
Gift of Bill Burke

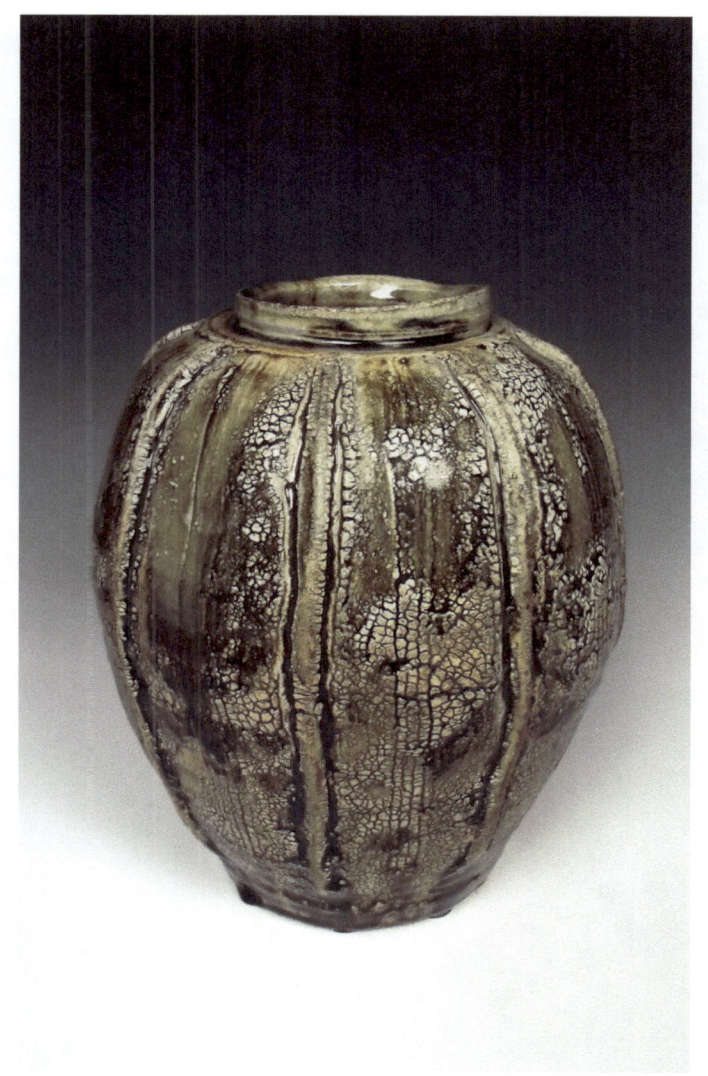

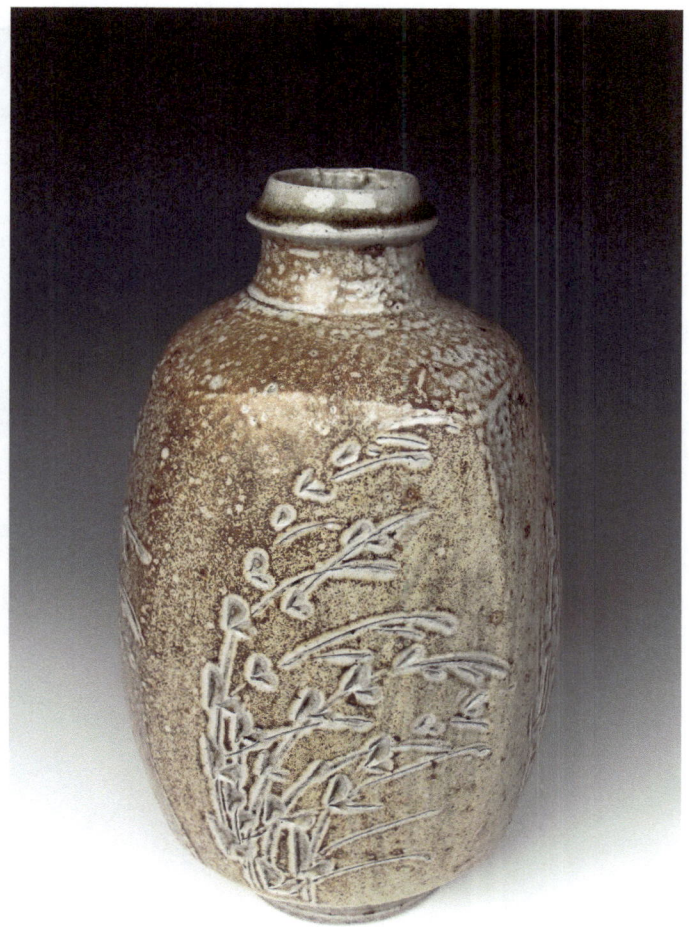

Mike Dodd, (b. 1943)
Ribbed Vases, 20th Century
Collection of Hannah & Russel Kully

Phil Rogers, (b. 1951)
Bottle, 20th Century
Collection of Heather & Chris Rupp

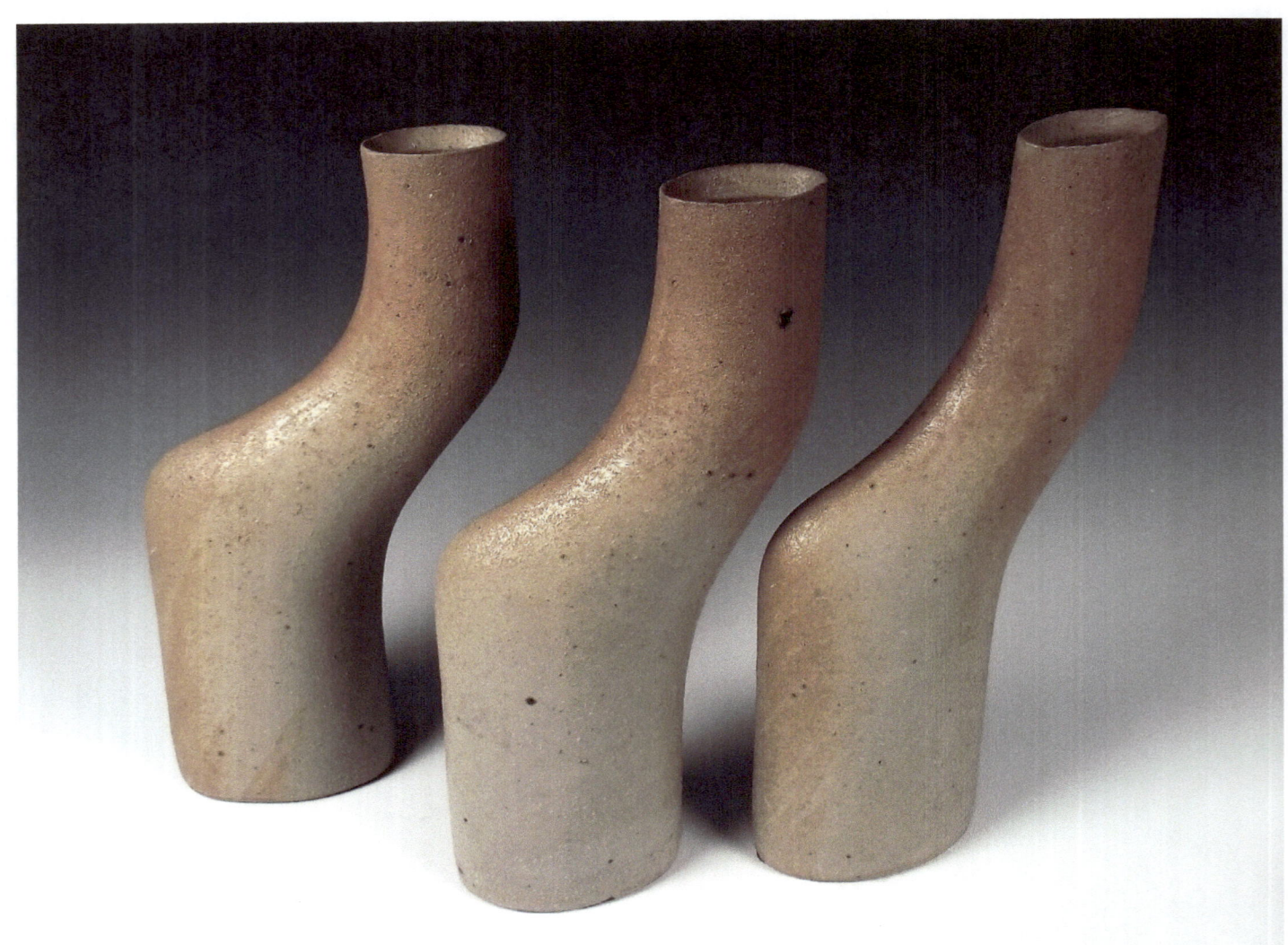

Joanna Constantinidis (1927-2000)
Sculpted Vessels, 20th Century
Collection of Lynn Myers

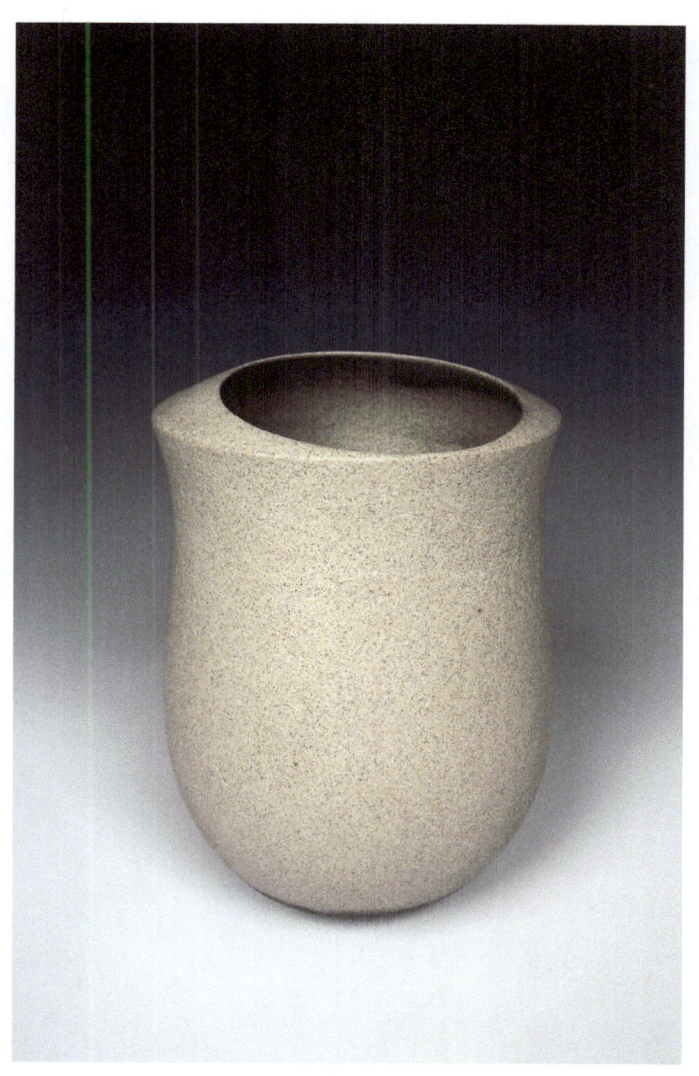

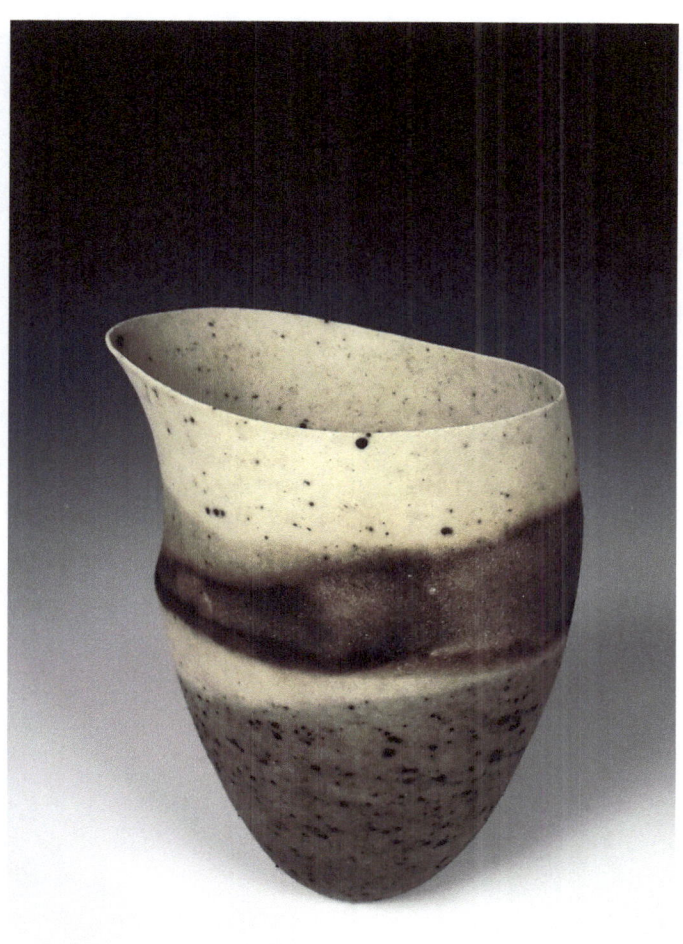

Jennifer Lee, (b. 1956)
Vessel, Late 20th Century
Collection of Sharon &
Paul Dauer

Jennifer Lee
Dark Pot With Haloed Ochre Bands, 2004
Collection of Jo Lauria &
Michael Fargo

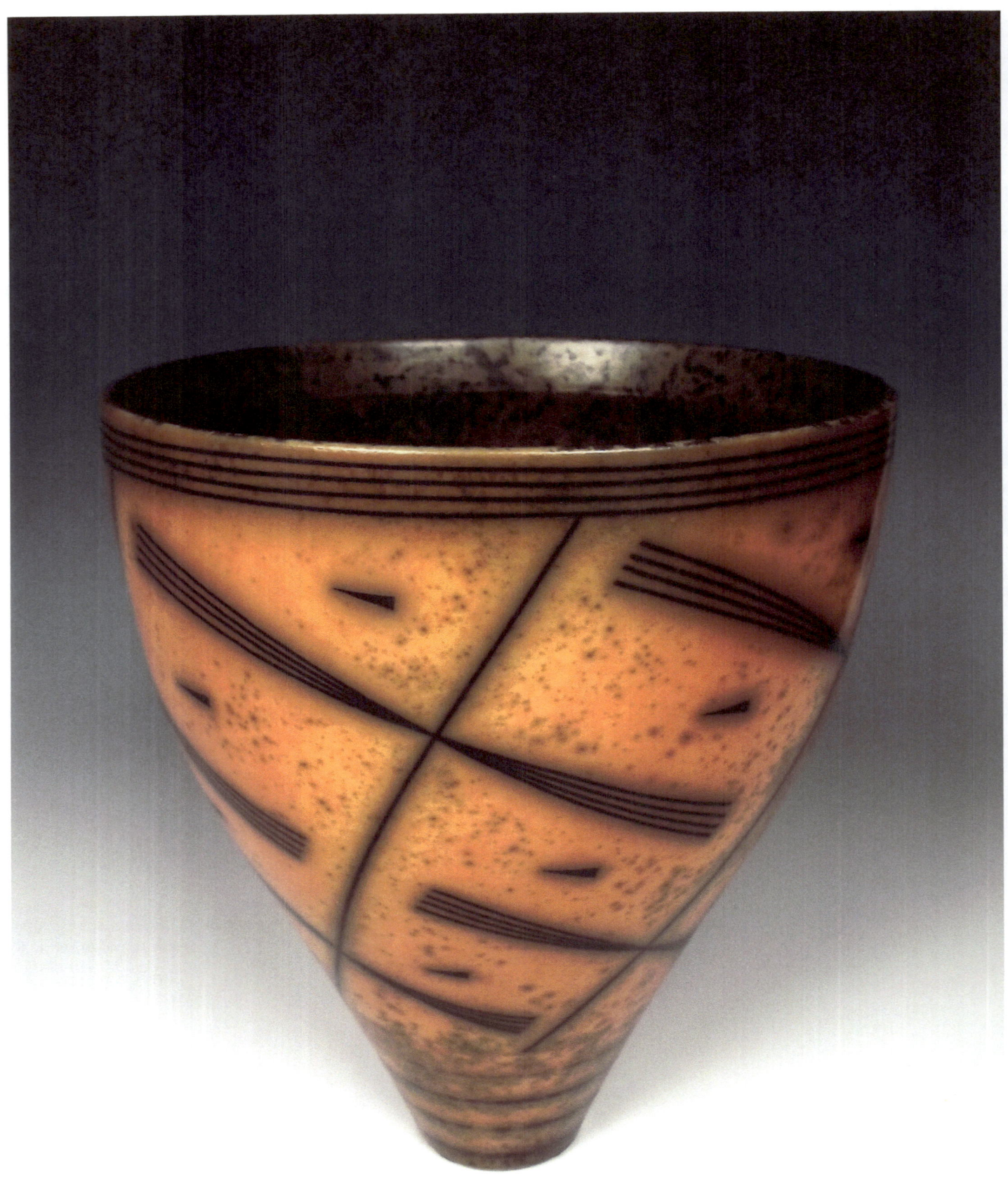

Left:
Duncan Ross, (b. 1950s)
Conical Form, 20th Century
AMOCA Permanent
Collection, Gift of Bill Burke

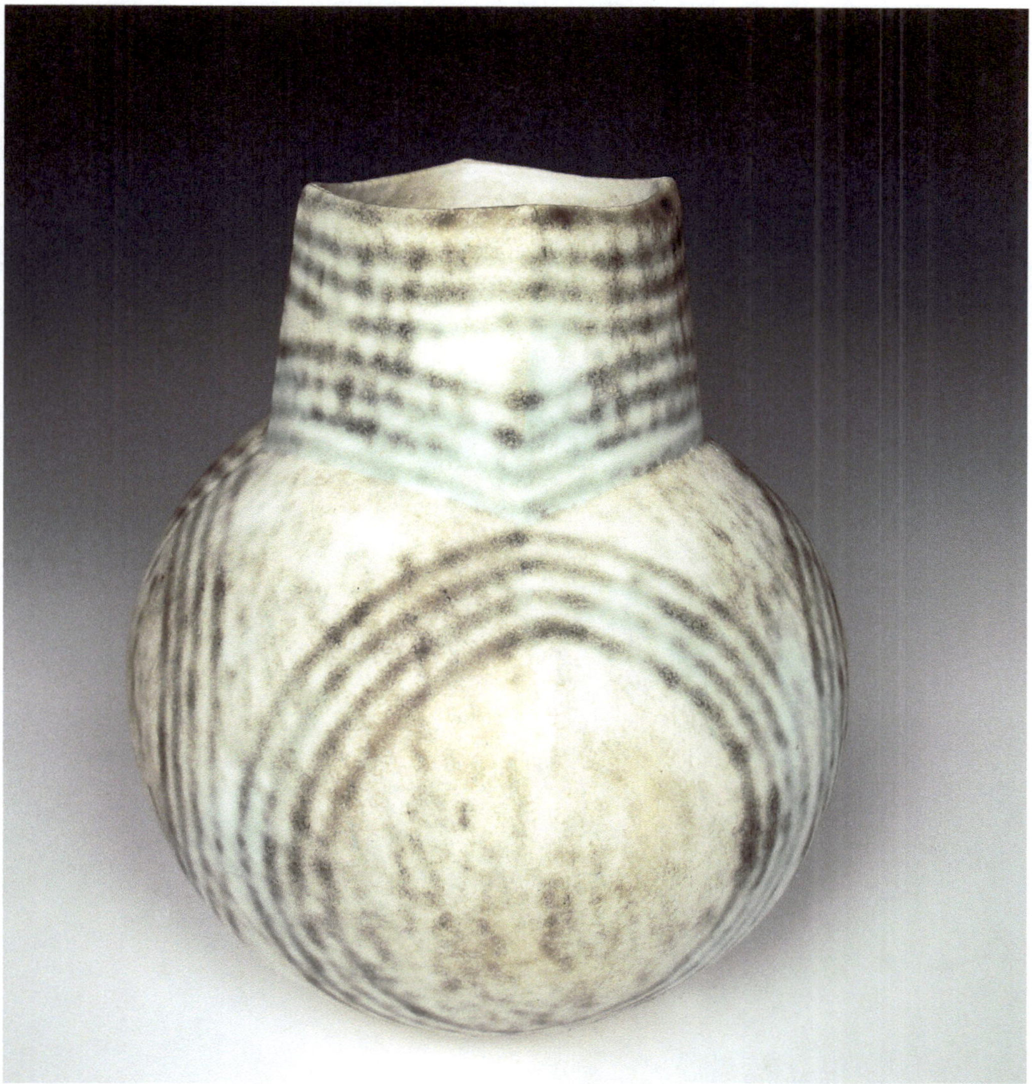

John Ward, (b. 1938)
Vessel, 20th Century
Collection of Hannah & Russel
Kully

Geoffrey Swindell, (b. 1944)
Sculpted Orb, c. 2000
AMOCA Permanent
Collection, Gift of Bill Burke

Geoffrey Swindell (b. 1944)
Sculpted Teapot, c. 2000
AMOCA Permanent
Collection, Gift of Bill Burke

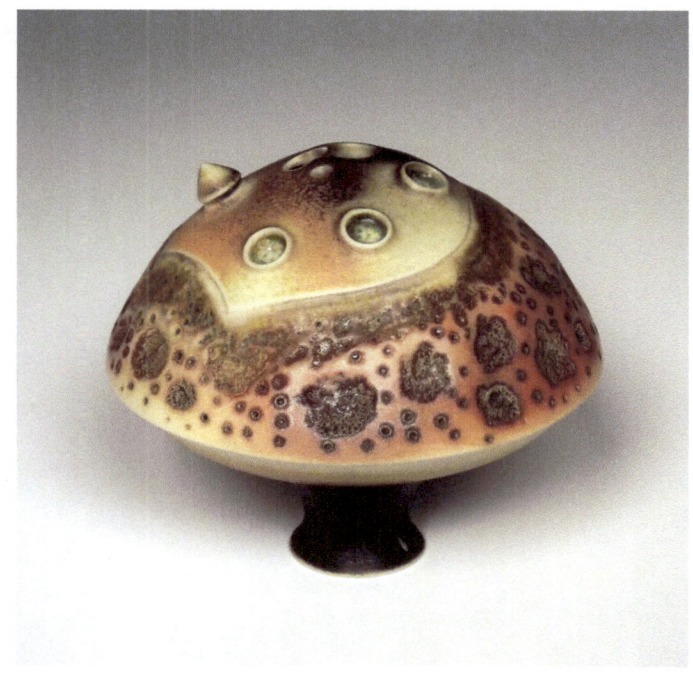

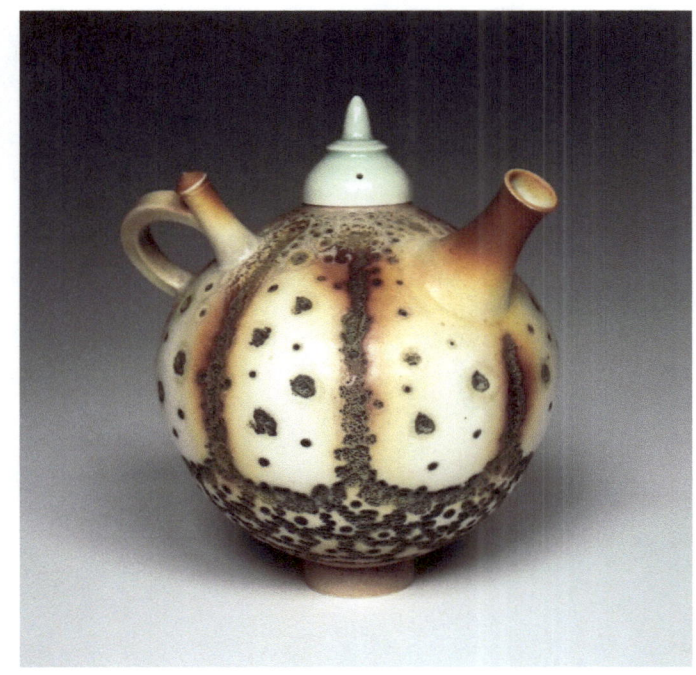

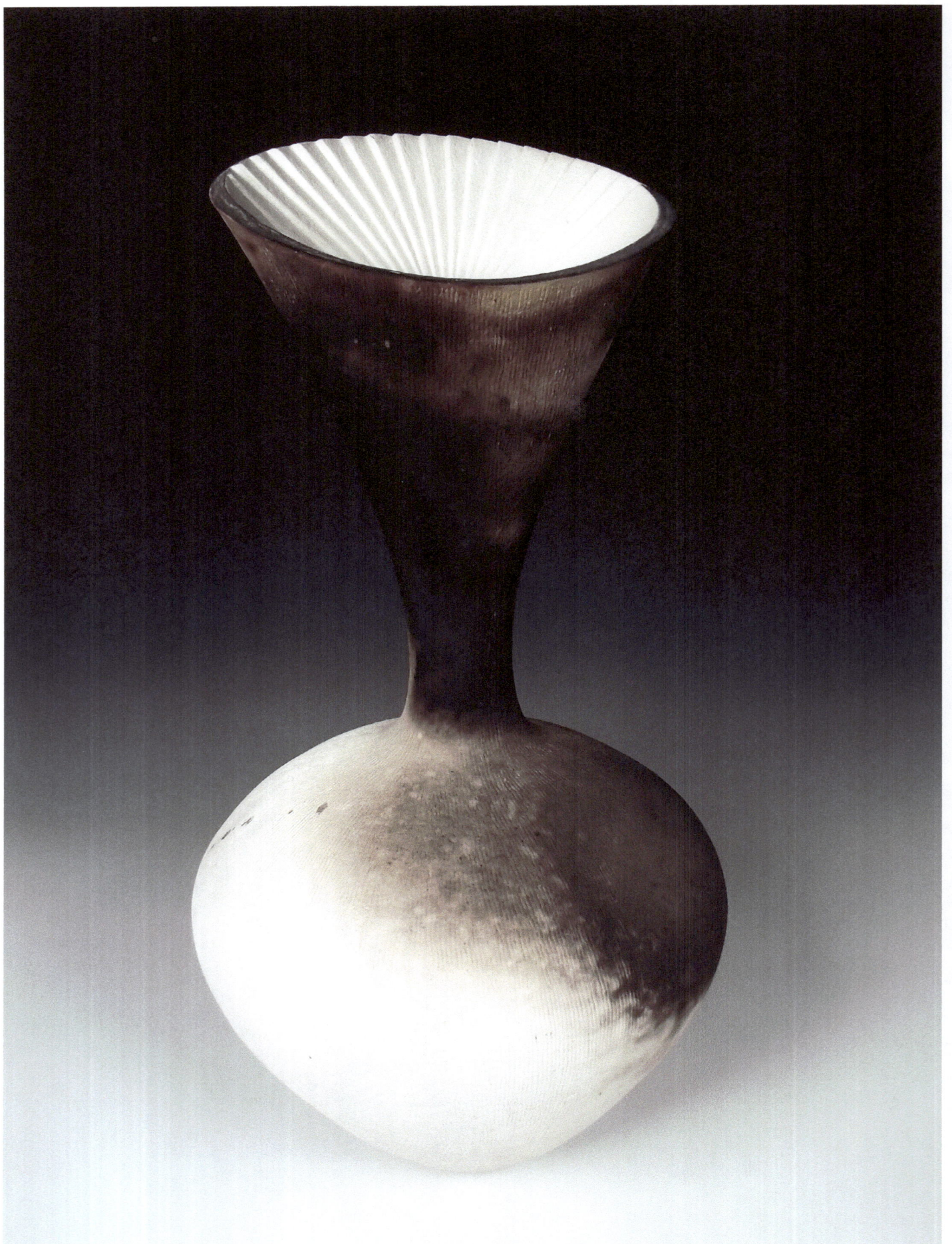

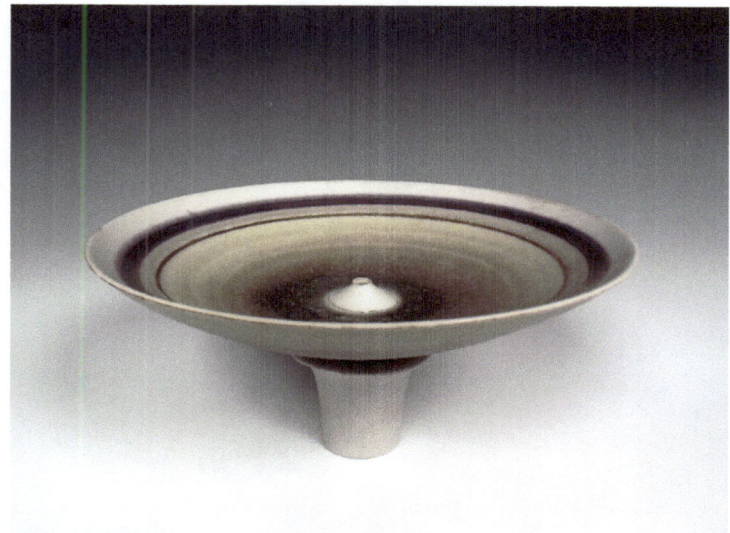

Left:
Glynn Hugo, (b. 1934)
Flared Vessel, 20th Cent.
Collection of Diane &
Igal Silber

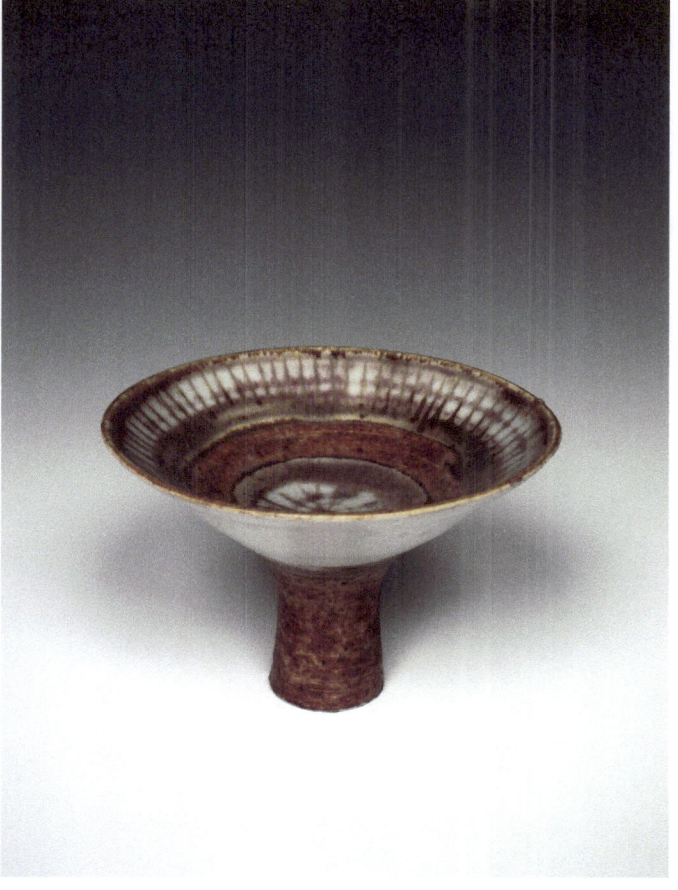

Right:
Marianne De Trey, (b. 1913)
Flared Bowl, Late 20th Cent.
Collection of Judy &
Richard Jacobs

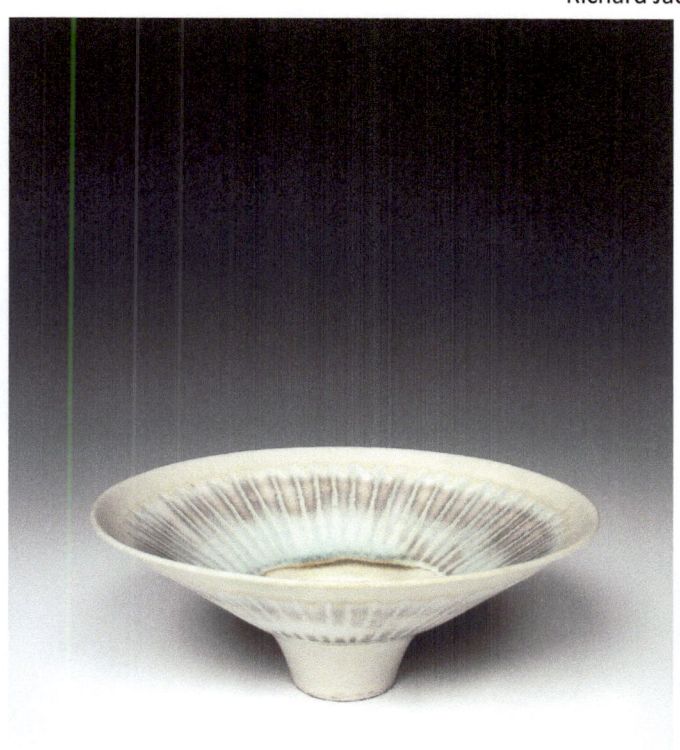

Left:
Peter Wills, (b. 1955)
Flared Bowl, c. 2000
Collection of Judy & Richard
Jacobs

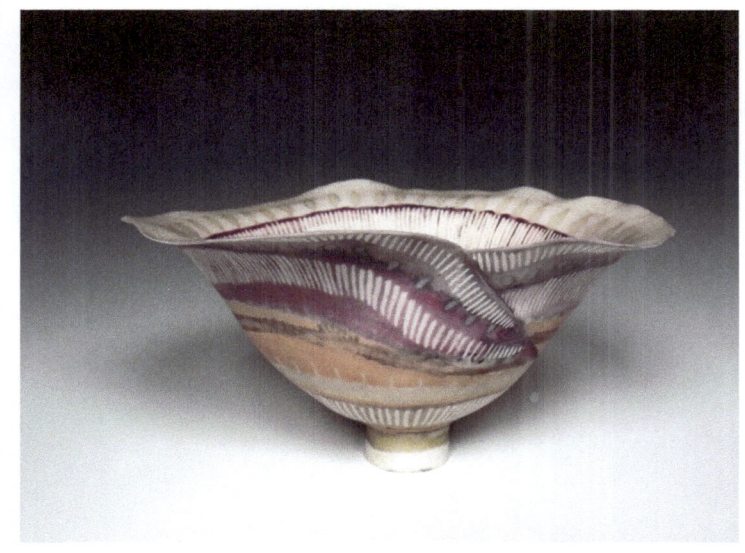

Left:
Judy Trim, (1943-2001)
Flare Necked Bottle, 1984
Collection of Diane & Igal Silber

Right:
Mary Rogers, (b. 1929)
Flared Bowl, 20th Cent.
Collection of Diane & Igal
Silber

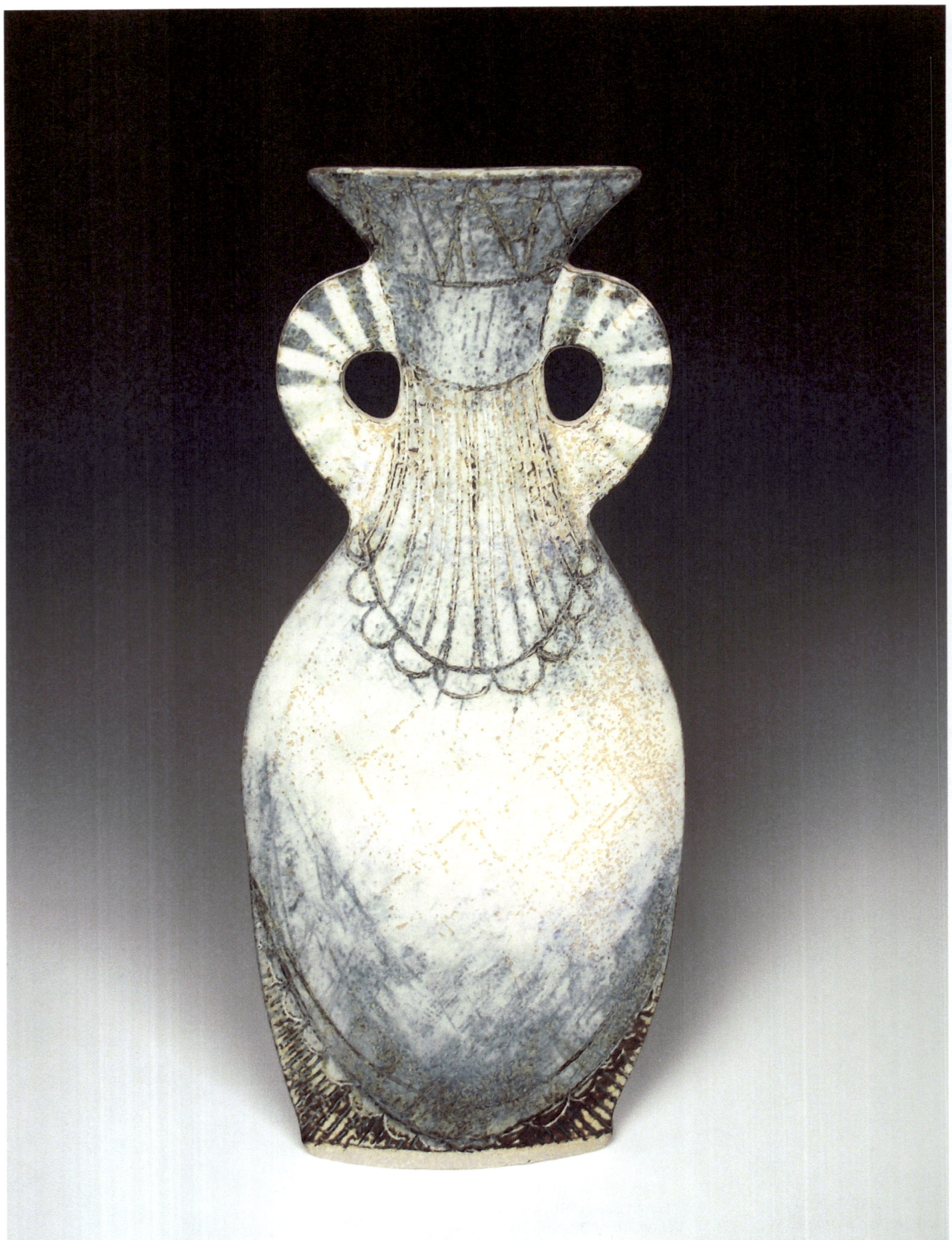

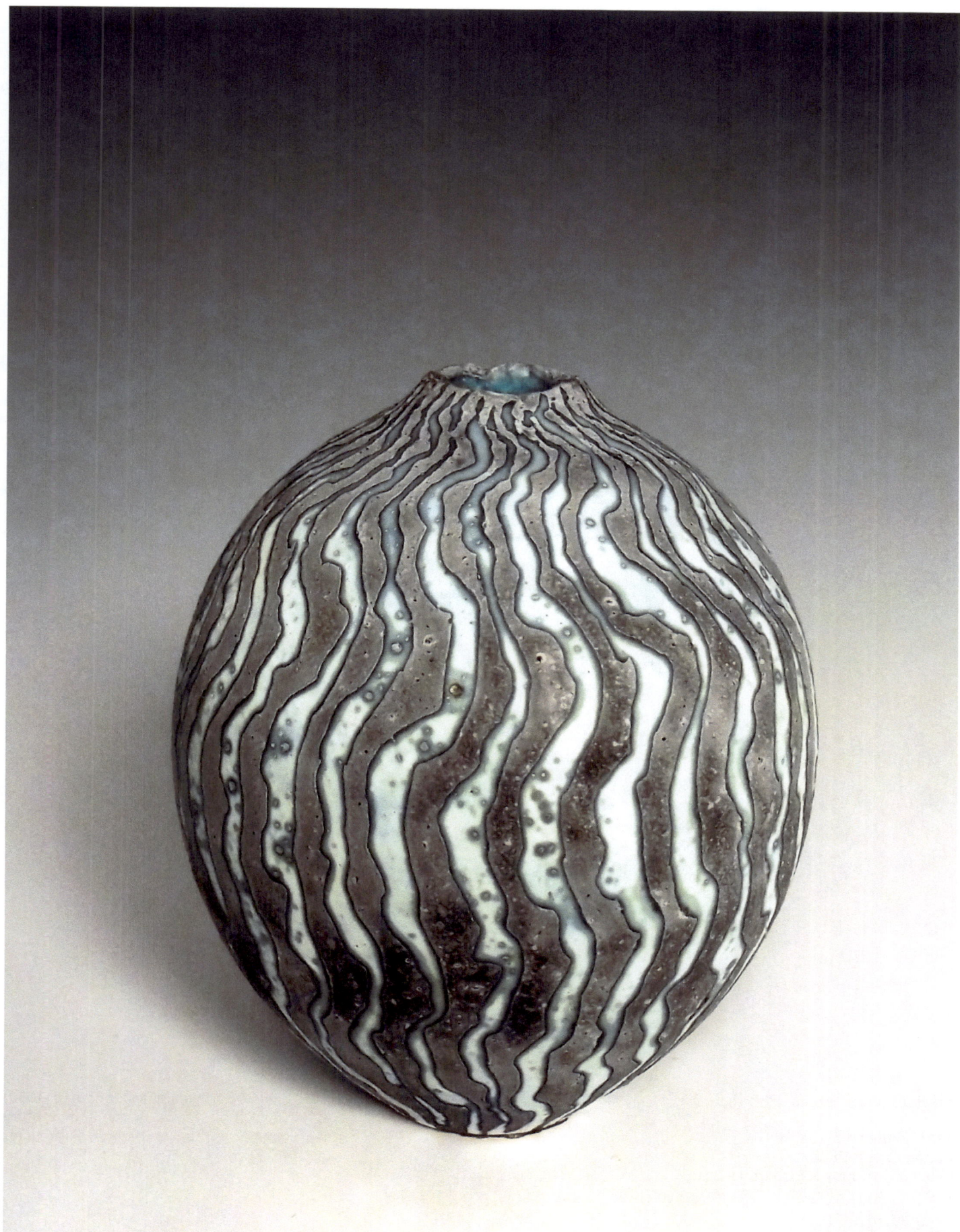

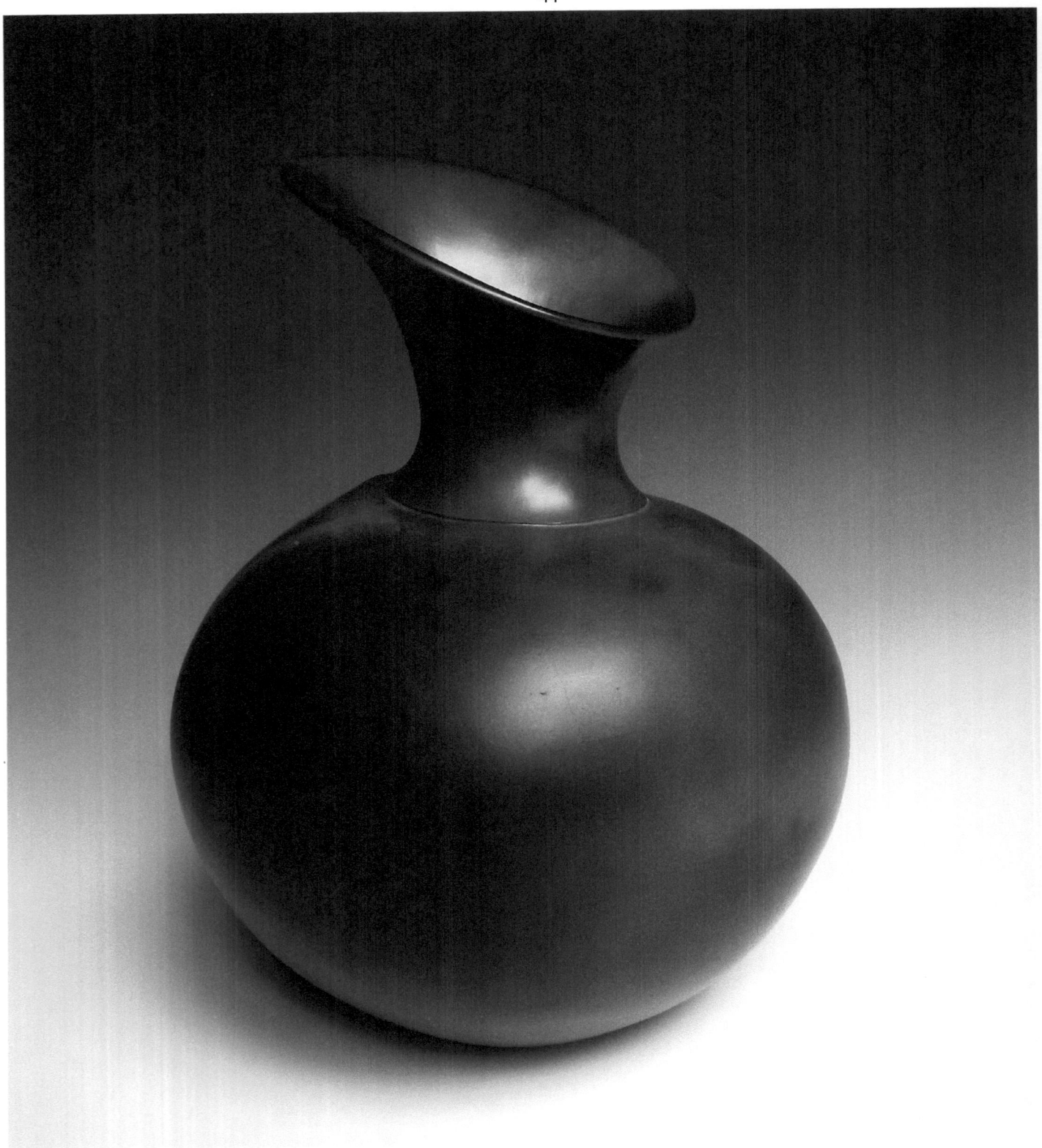

Previous pages spread left & right:

Terri Holman, (b. 1961)
Bottle, Late 20th Cent.
Collection of Judy & Richard Jacobs

Peter Beard, (b. 1951)
Bulbous Form, c. 2000
Collection of Judy & Richard Jacobs

Magdalena Odundo, (b. 1950)
Vase, 20th Century
Collection of Sharon & Paul Dauer

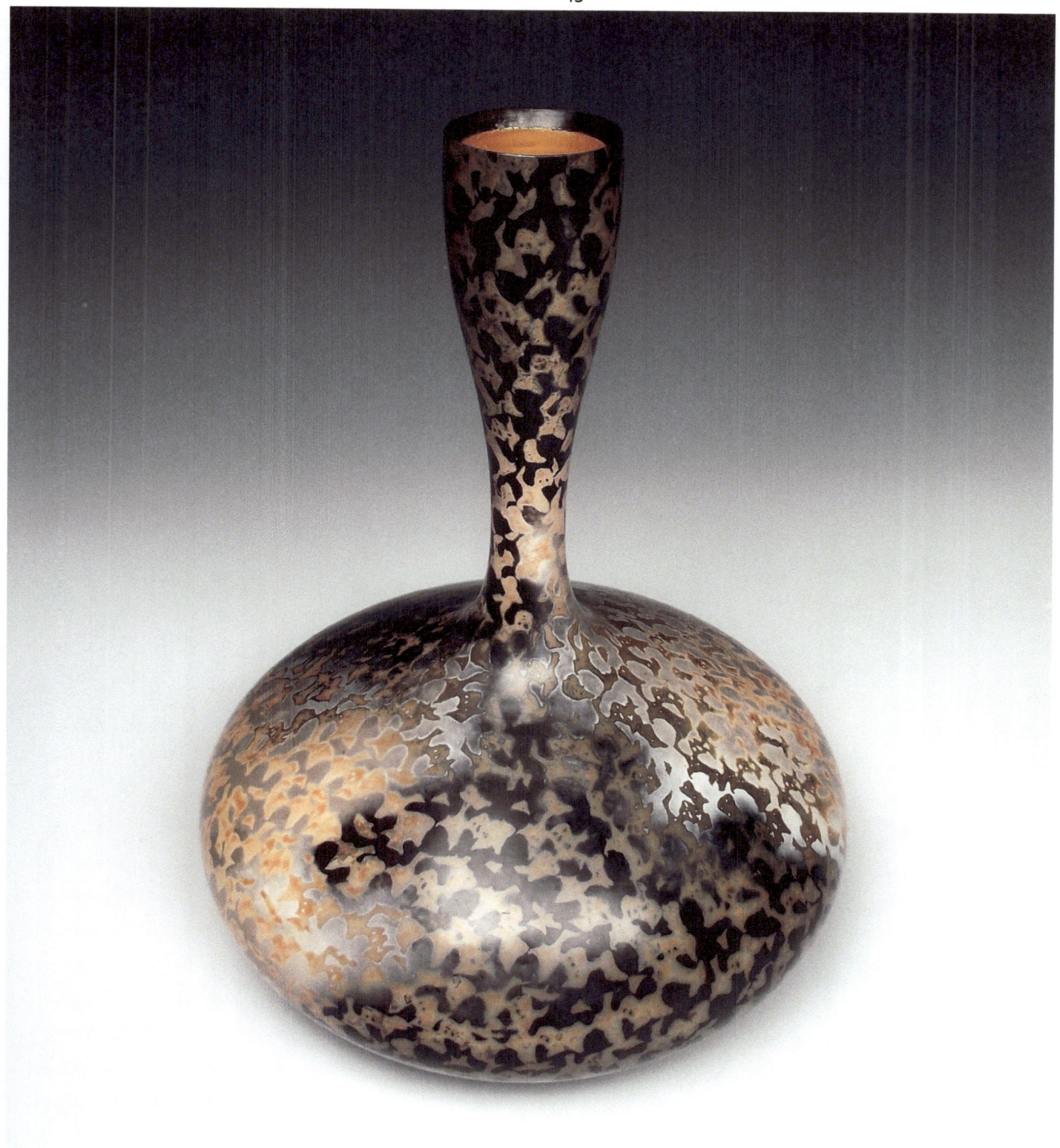

Duncan Ayscough, (b. 1961)
Bottle, Late 20th Century
Collection of Judy & Richard Jacobs

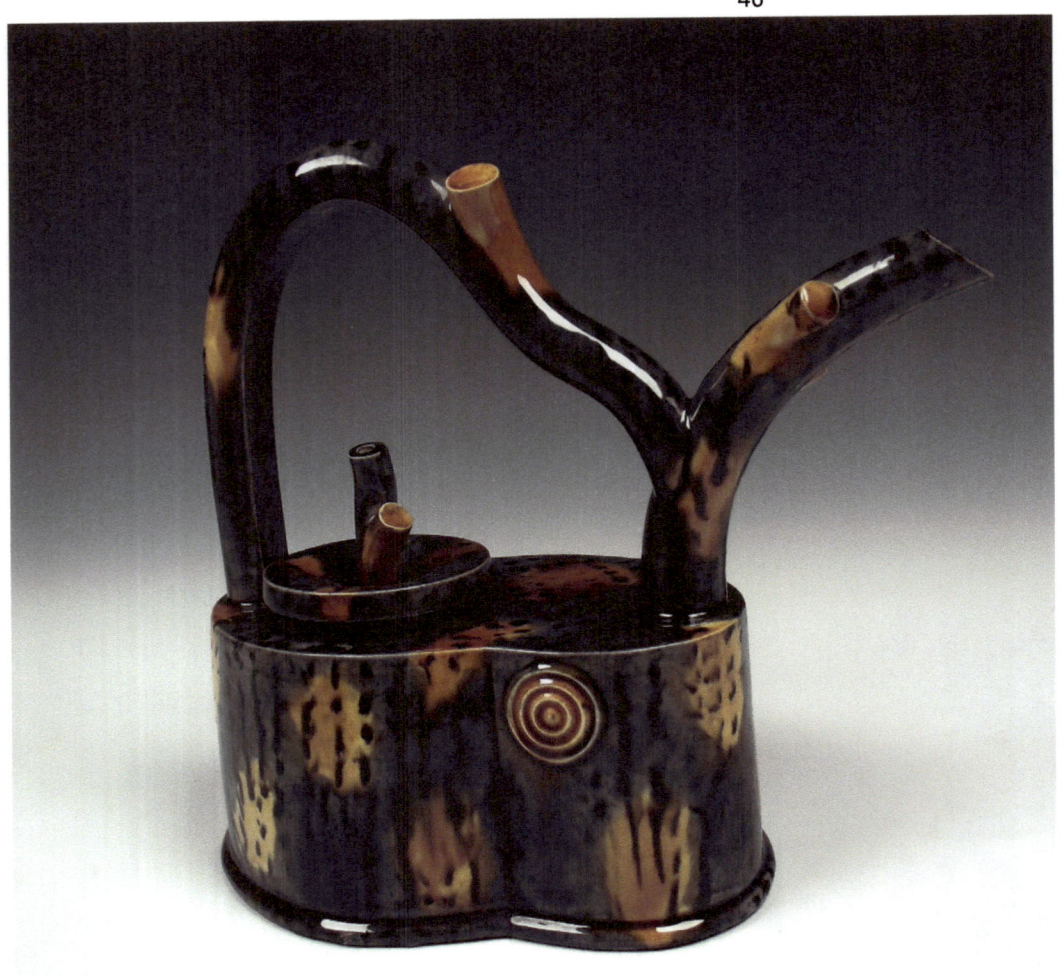

Walter Keeler, (b. 1942)
Teapot, 20th Century
Collection of Hannah &
Russel Kully

Alan Caiger-Smith, (b. 1930)
Bowl, 20th Century
Collection of Hannah &
Russel Kully

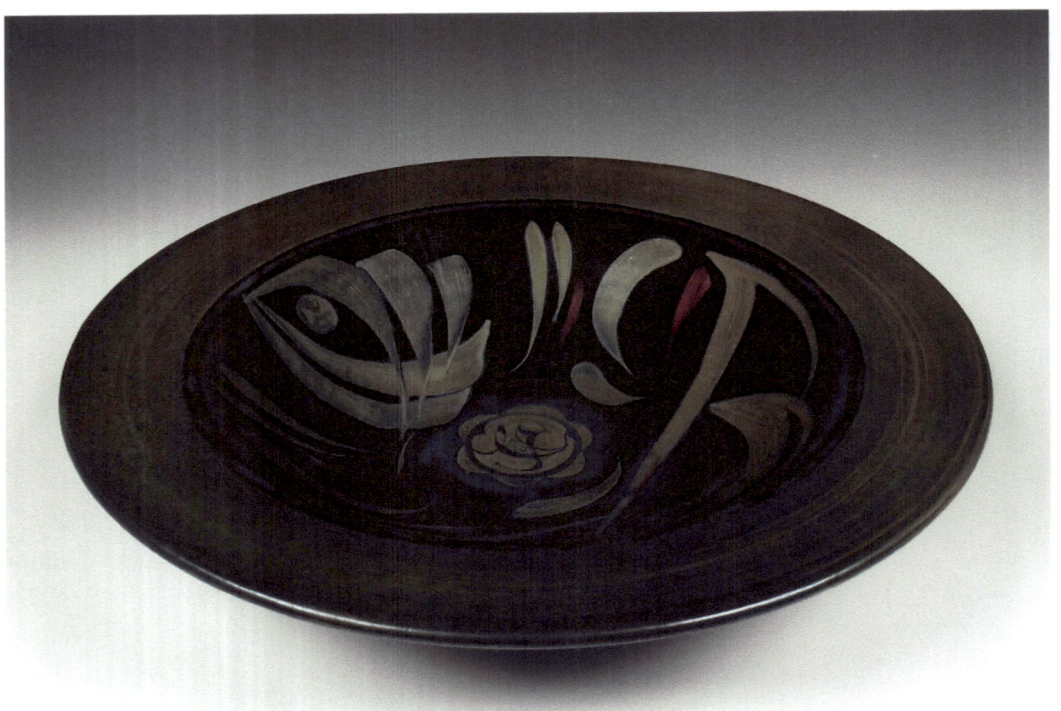

Right:
Linda Gunn-Russell,
(b. 1953)
Tea Pot, Late 20th Cent.
Collection of Lynn Myers

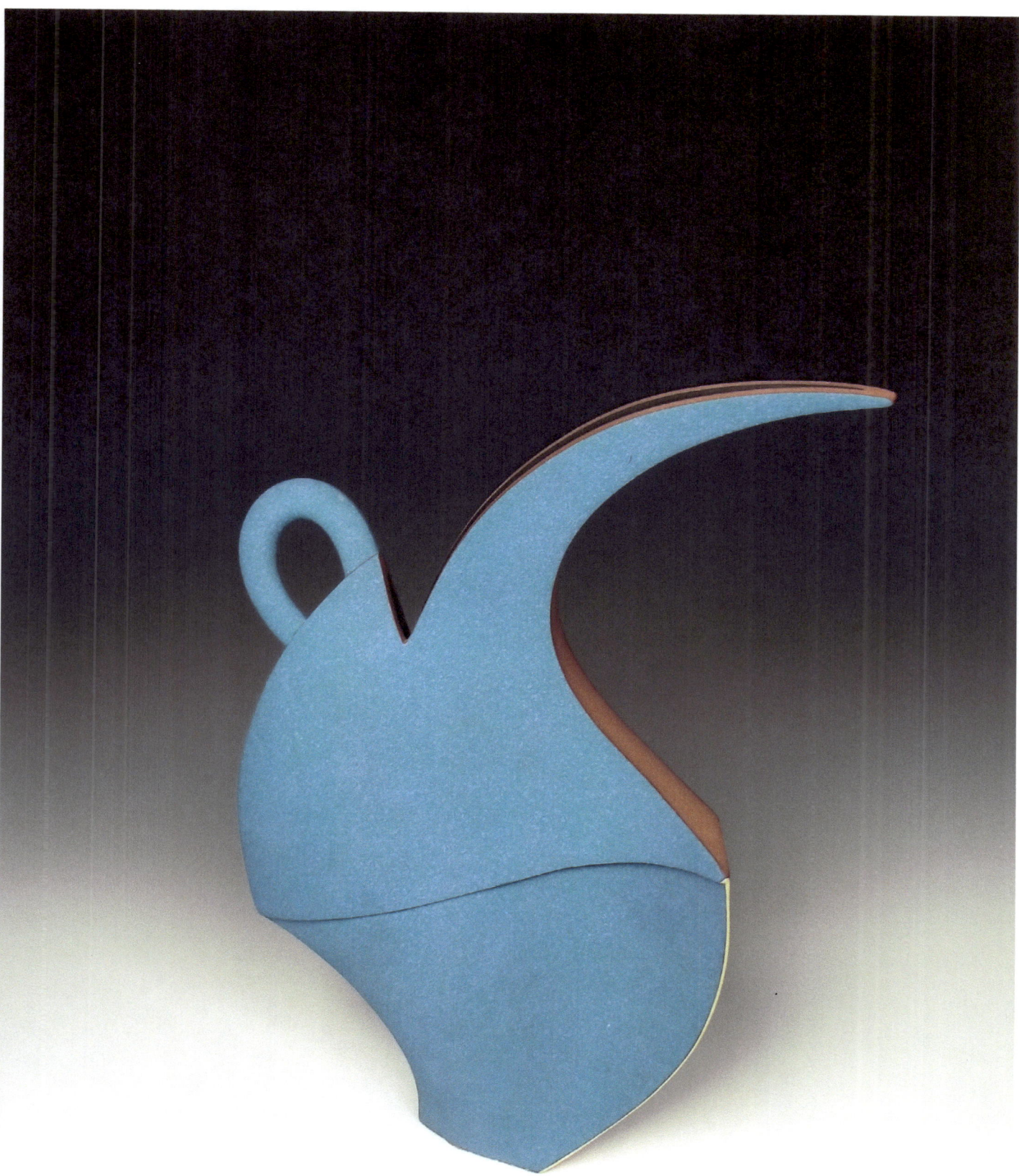

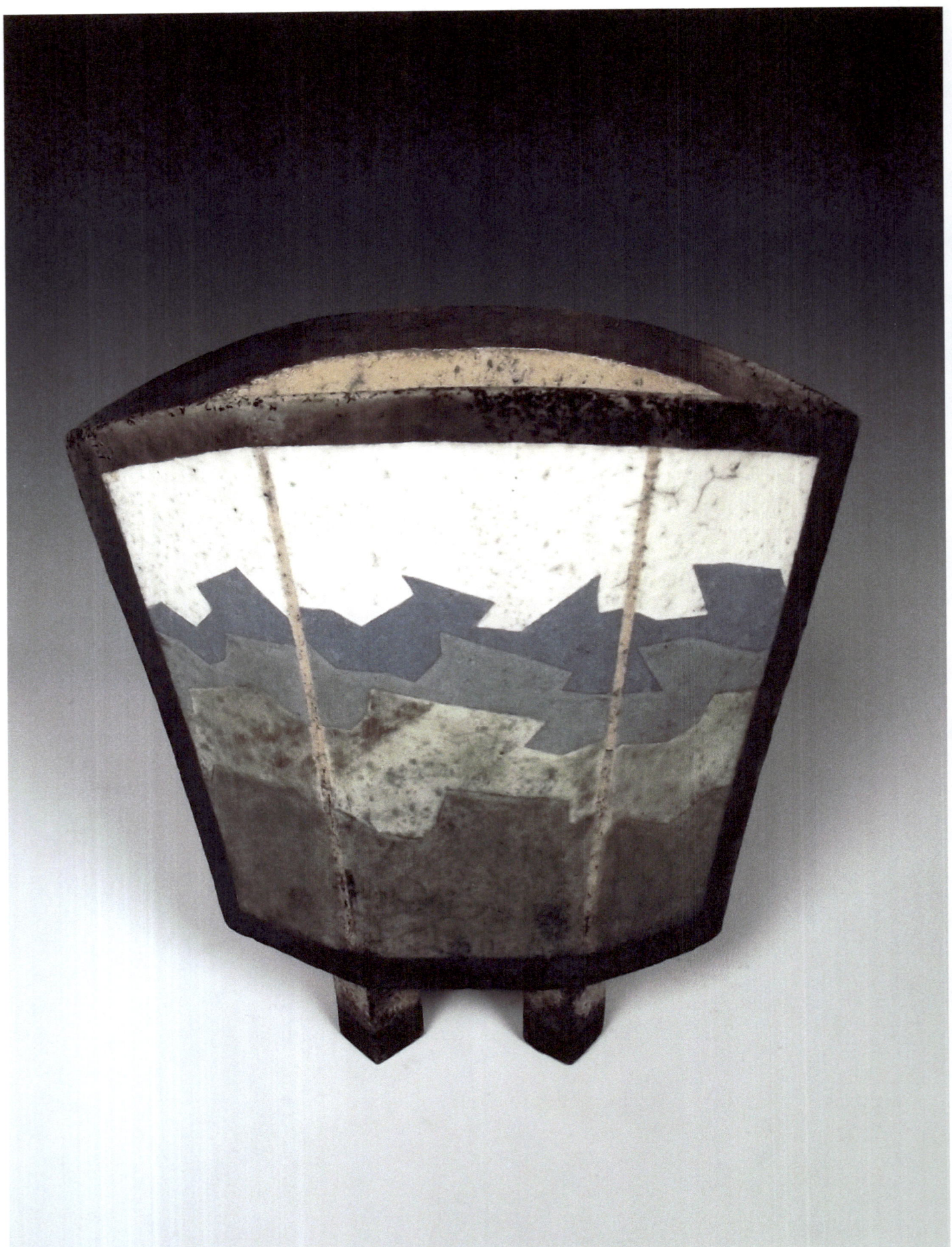

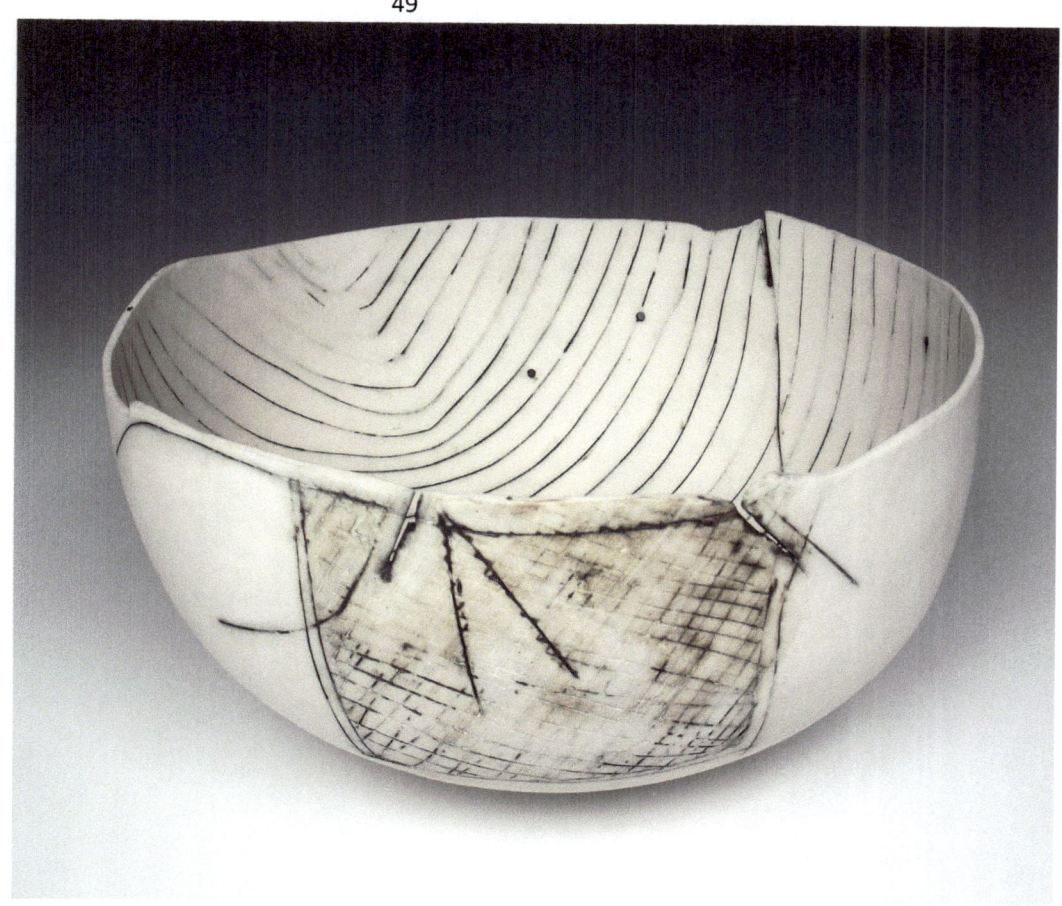

Gordon Baldwin, (b. 1932)
Bowl, 1984
Collection of Diane &
Igal Silber

Colin Pearson, (1923-2007)
Footed Vessel, 1983
Collection of Diane &
Igal Silber

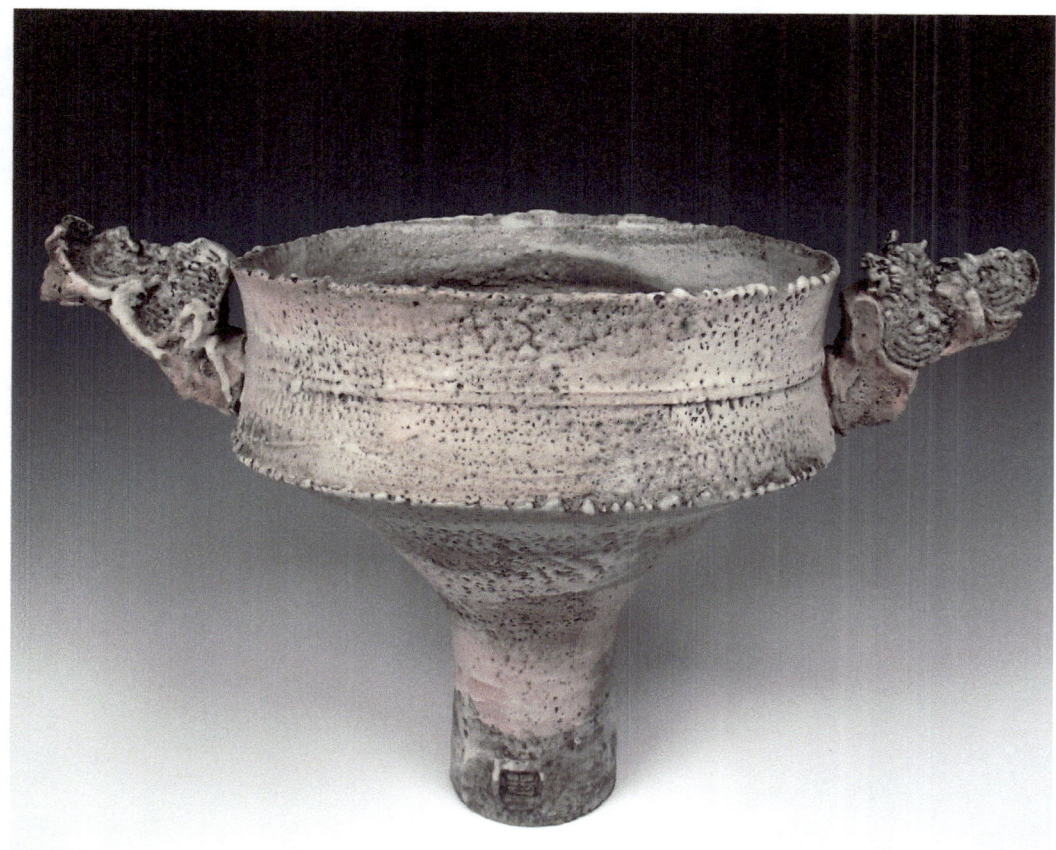

Left:
Elizabeth Raeburn
(b. 1943)
Sculptural Form, 1982
Collection of Diane &
Igal Silber

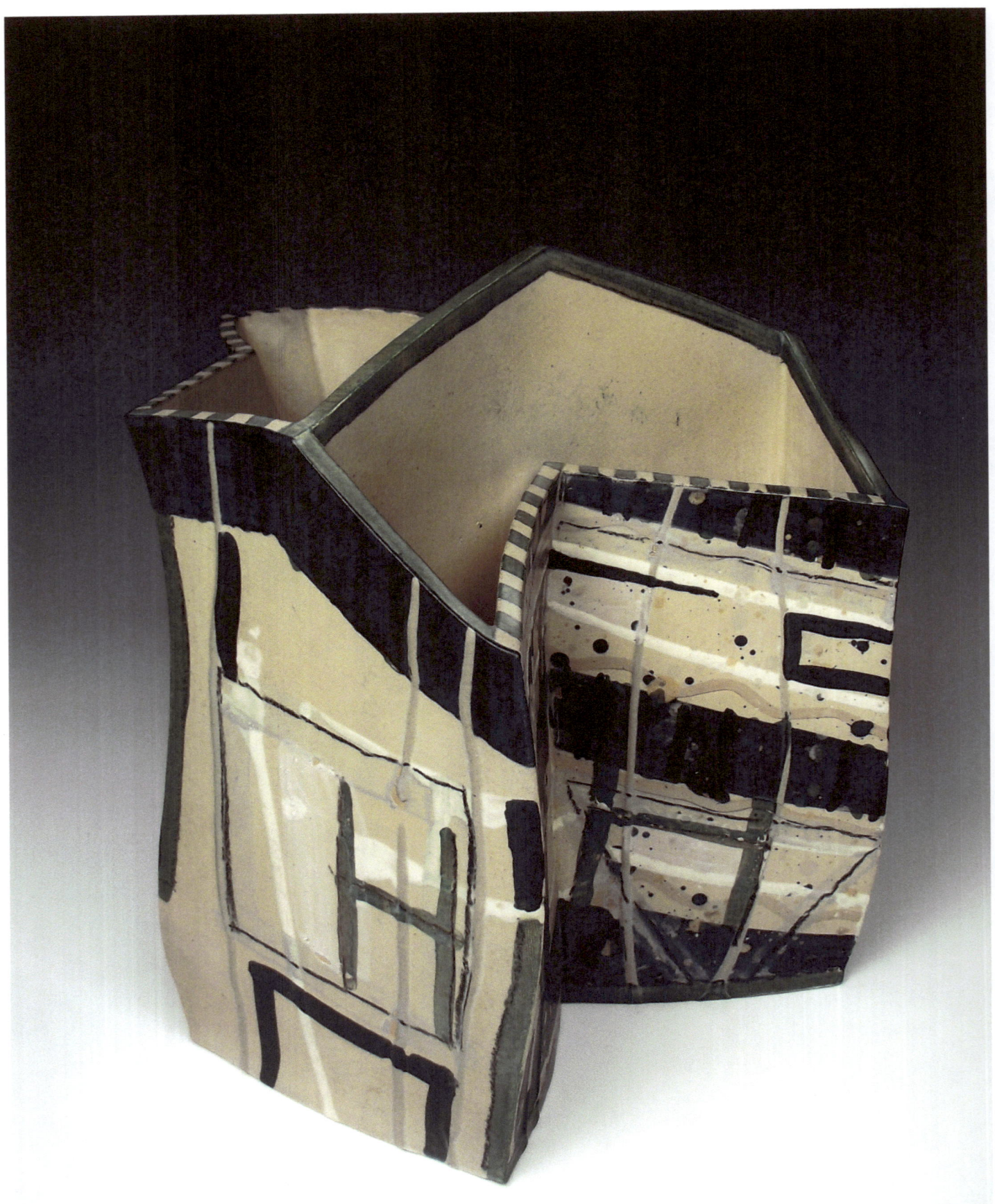

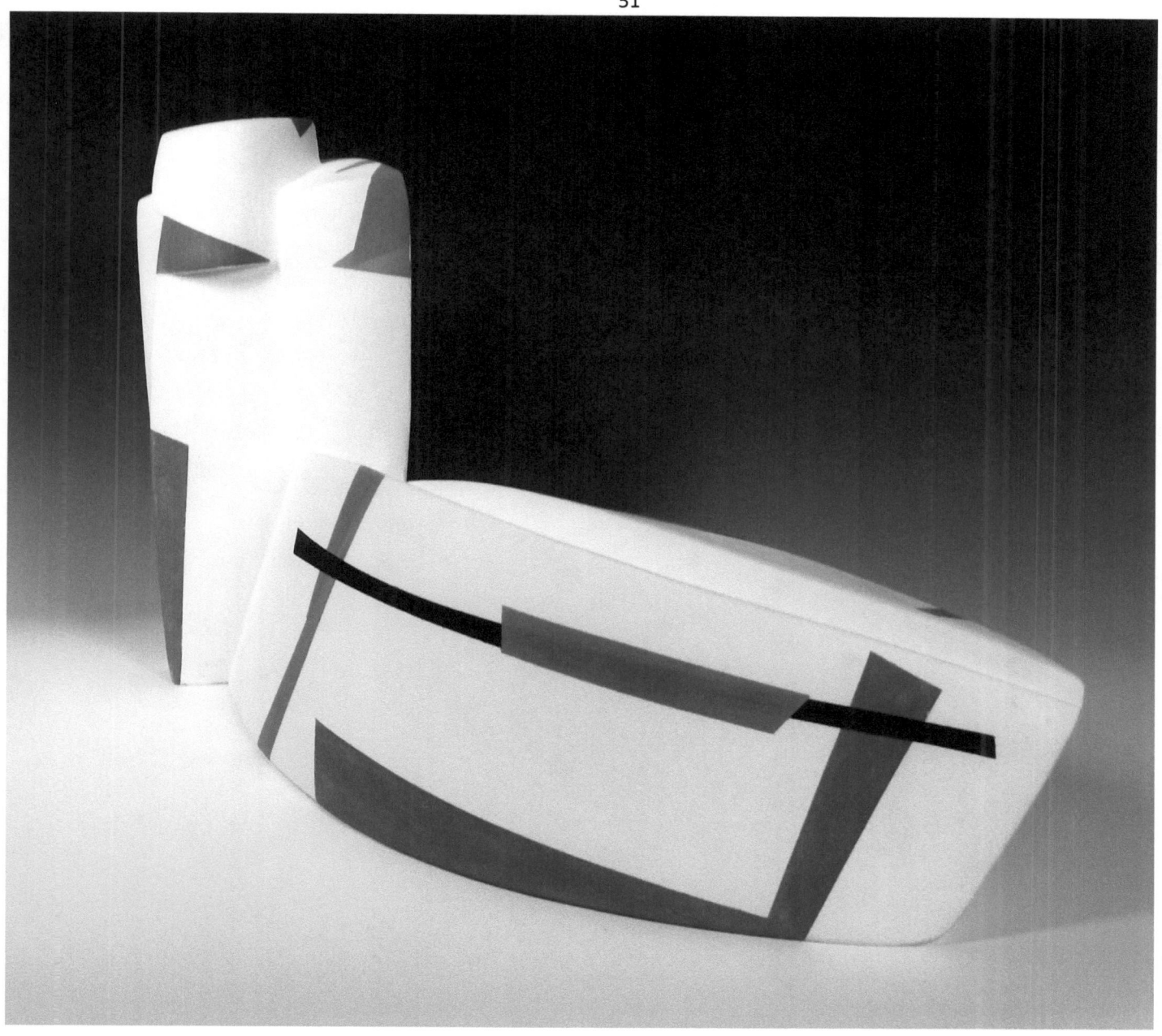

Michael Moore, (b. 1968)
Sculpture, 2010
Collection of Sharon &
Paul Dauer

Left:
Alison Britton, (b. 1948)
Big Green Pot, 1982
Collection of Diane & Igal Silber

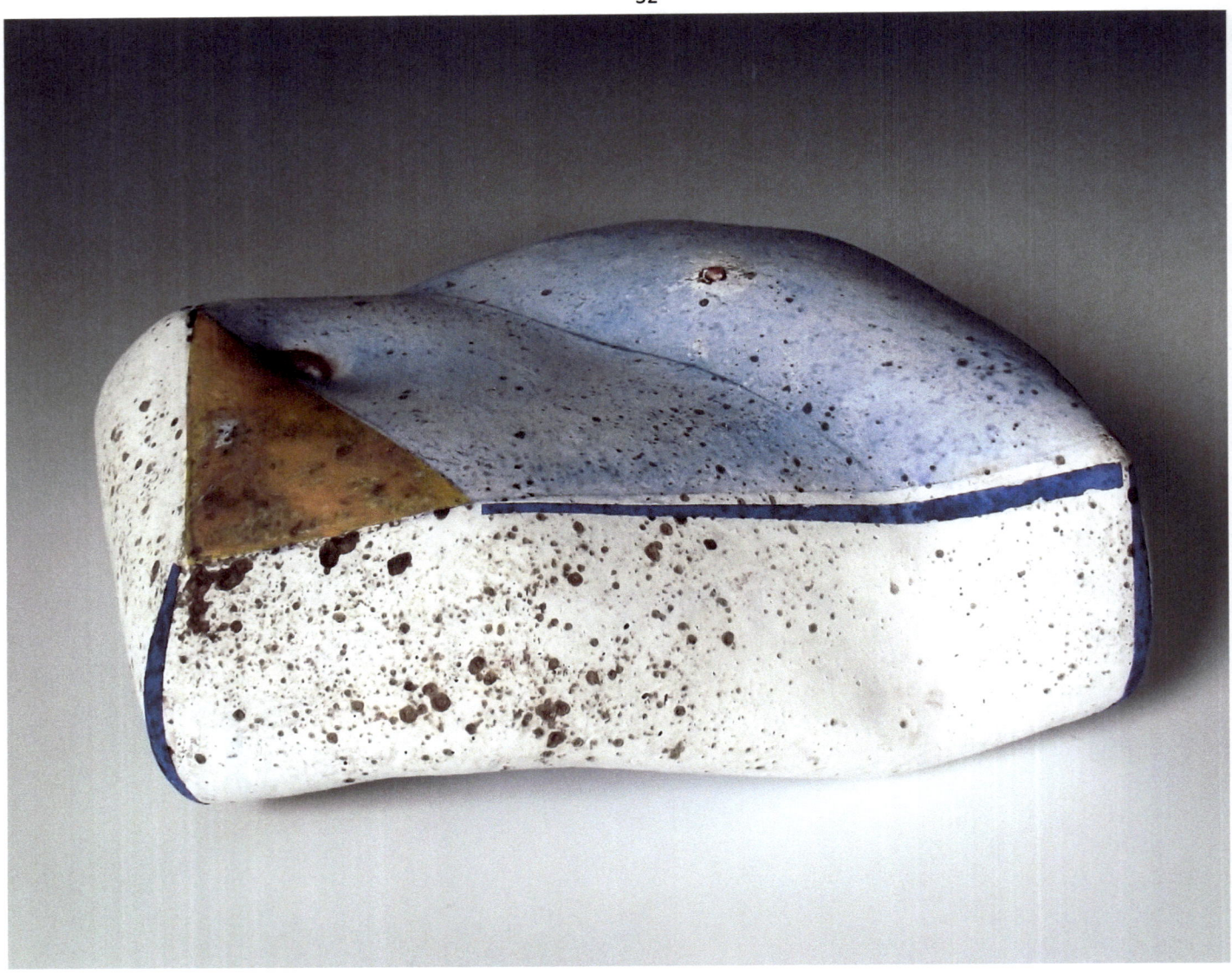

Regina Heinz, (b. 1957)
Pillow Form, Late 20th Century
Collection of Sharon & Paul Dauer

Martin Smith, (b. 1950)
Vessel, c. 1985
Collection of Jo Lauria & Mi-
chael Fargo

Martin Smith
Surface and Void No. 3, 20th
Century
Collection of Lynn Myers

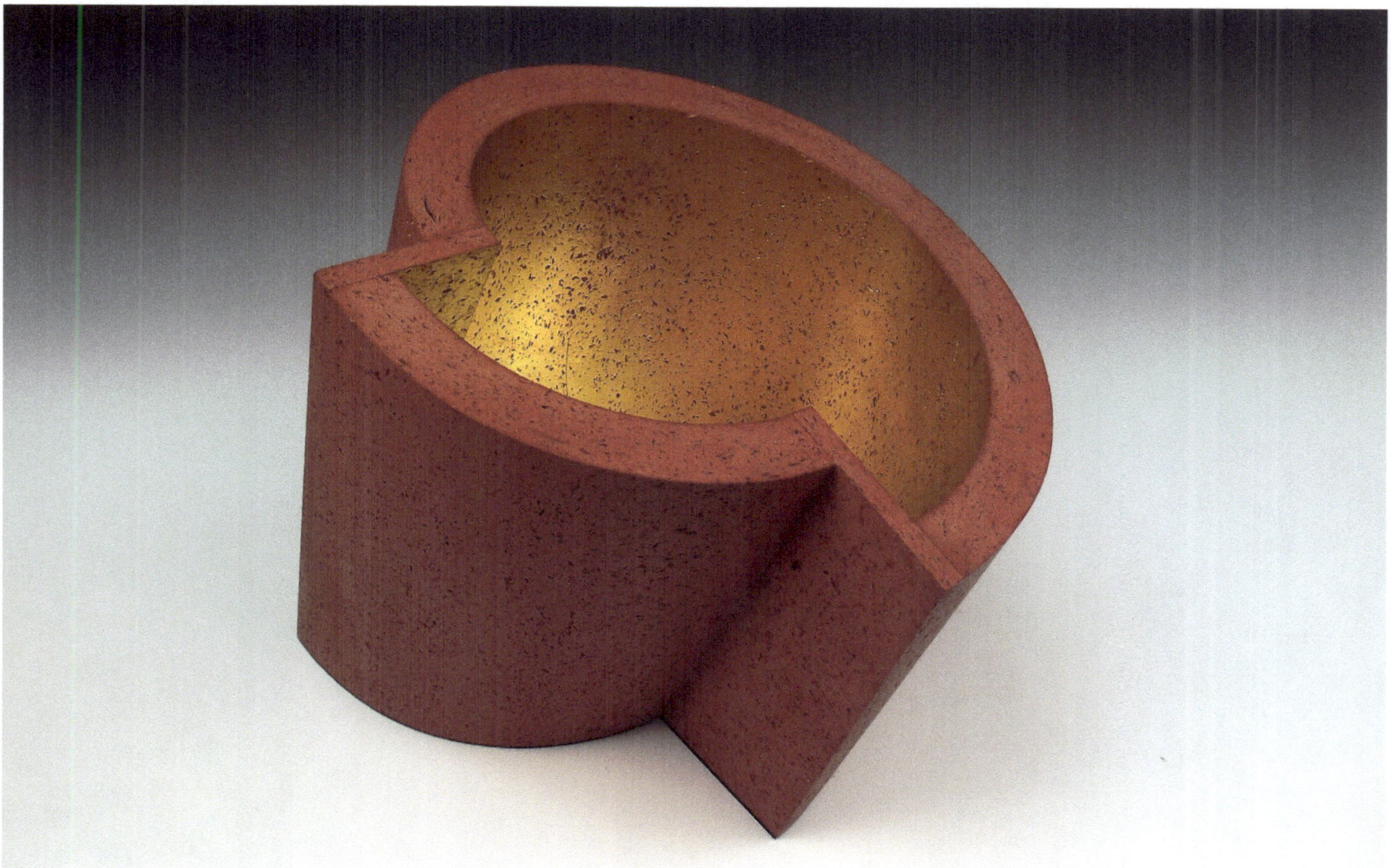

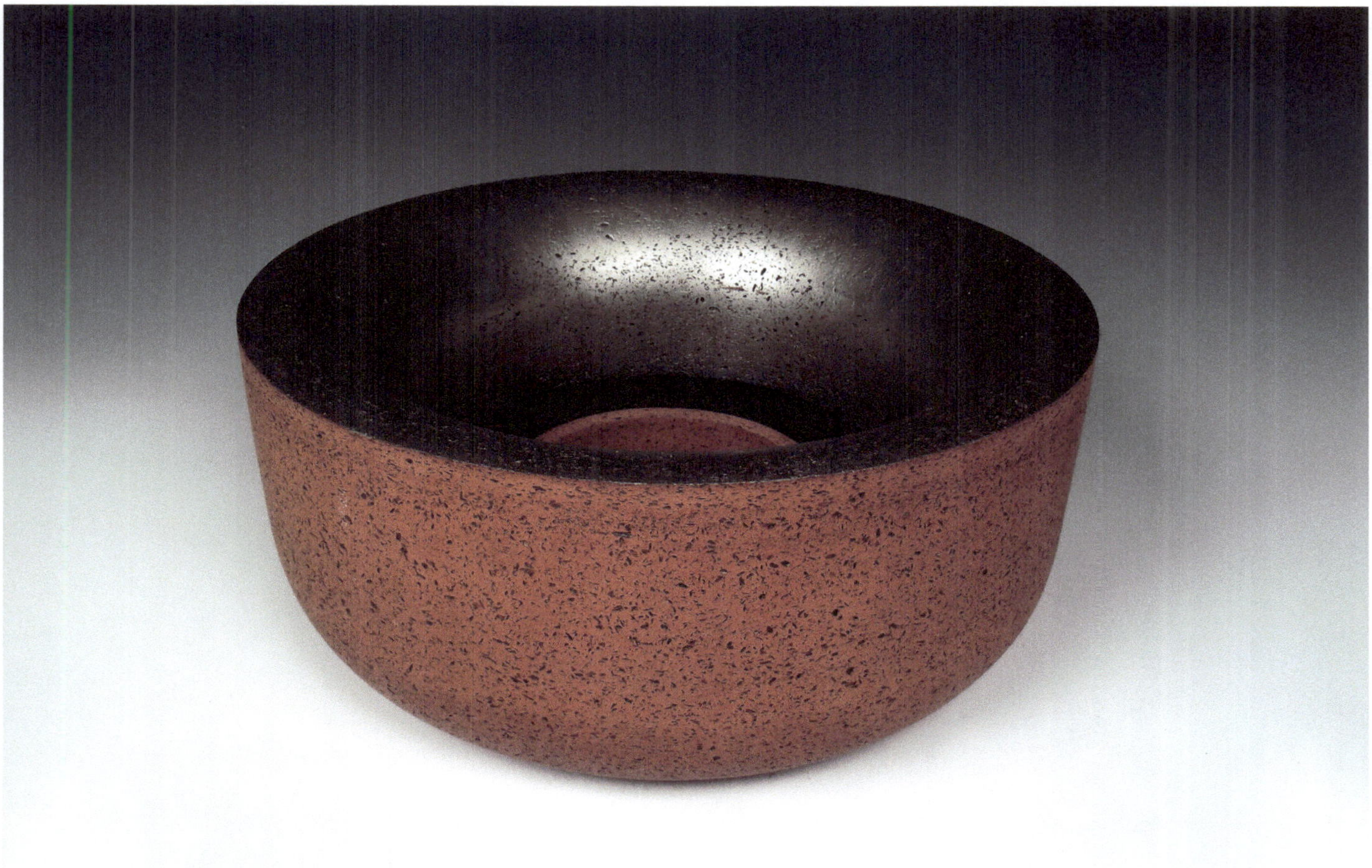

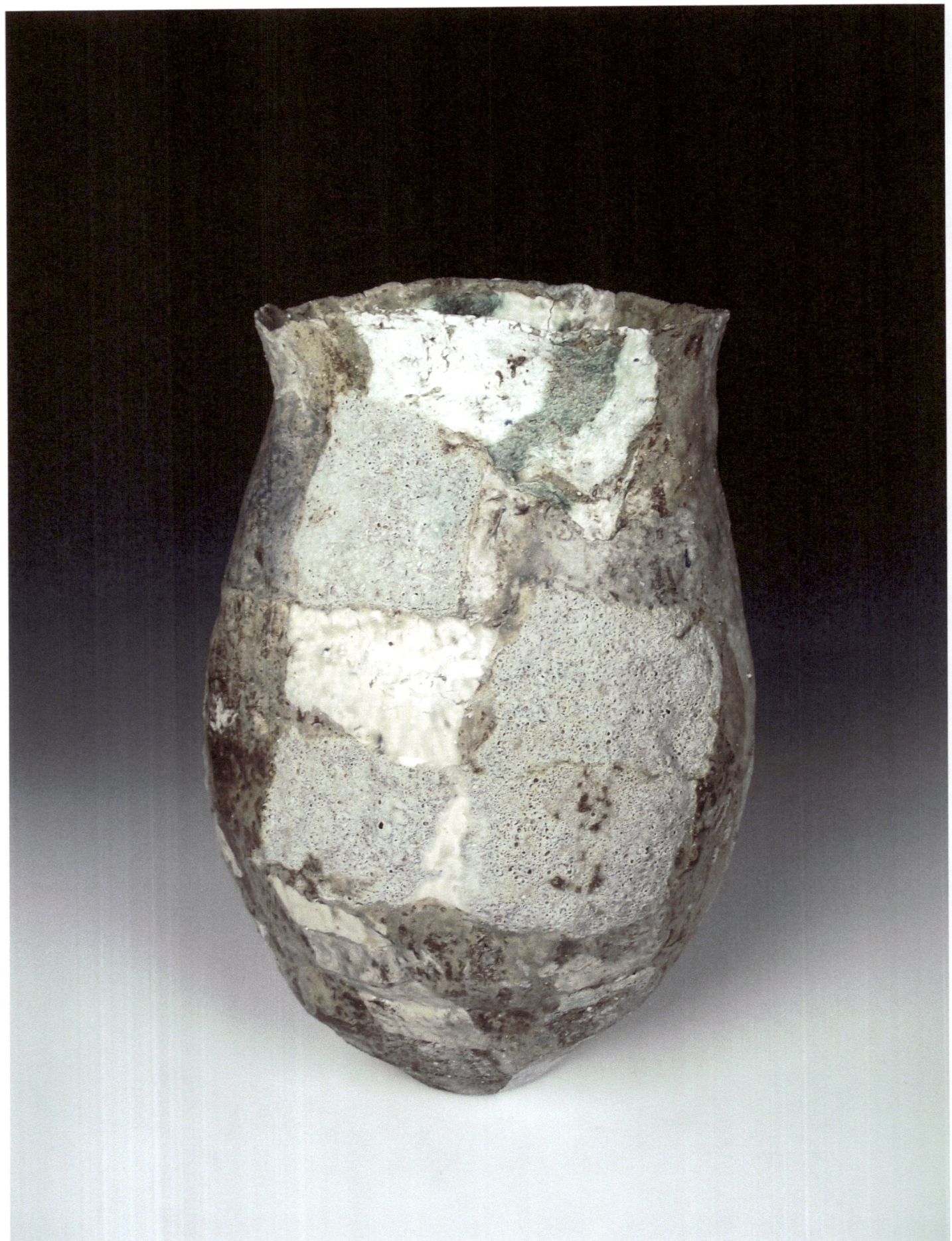

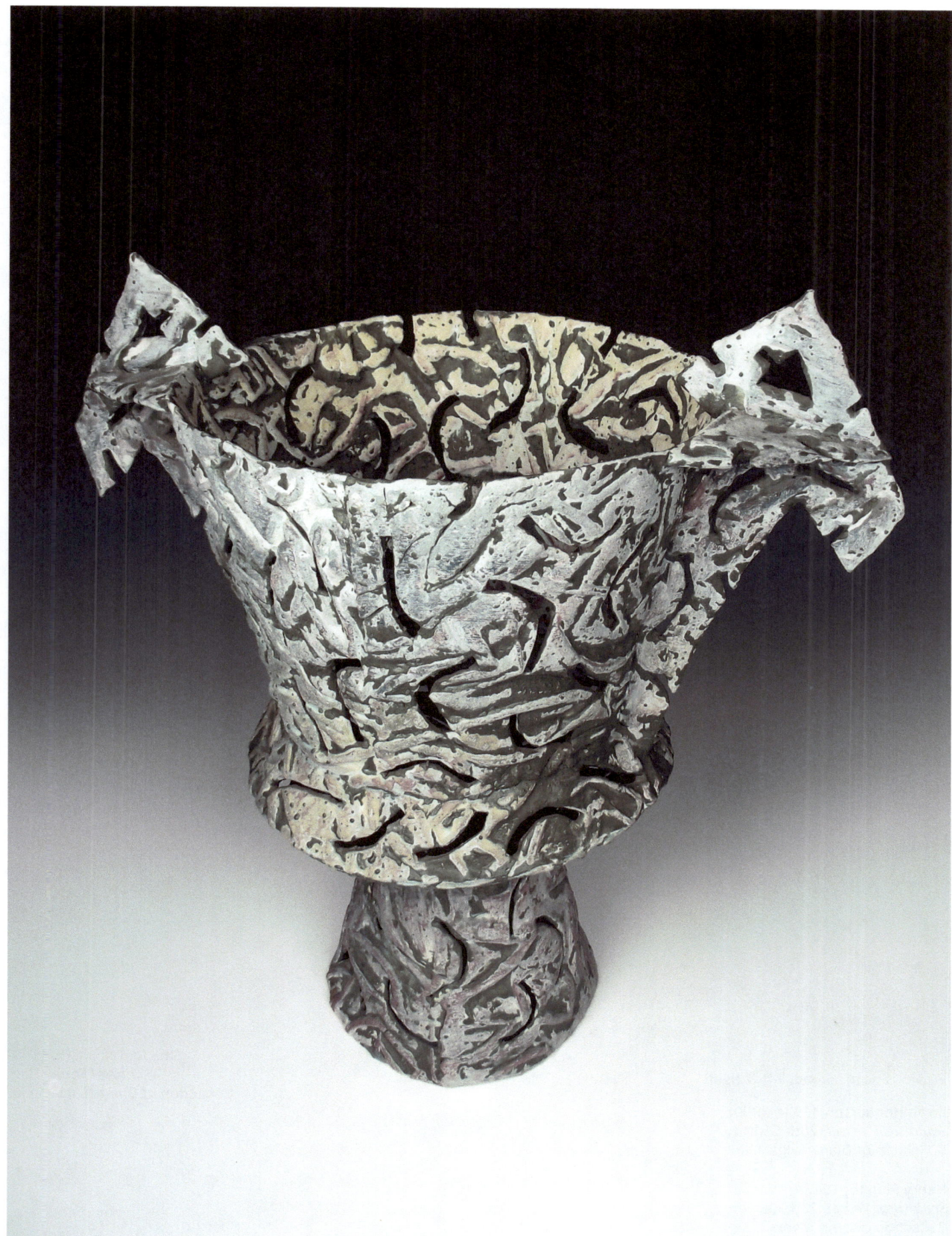

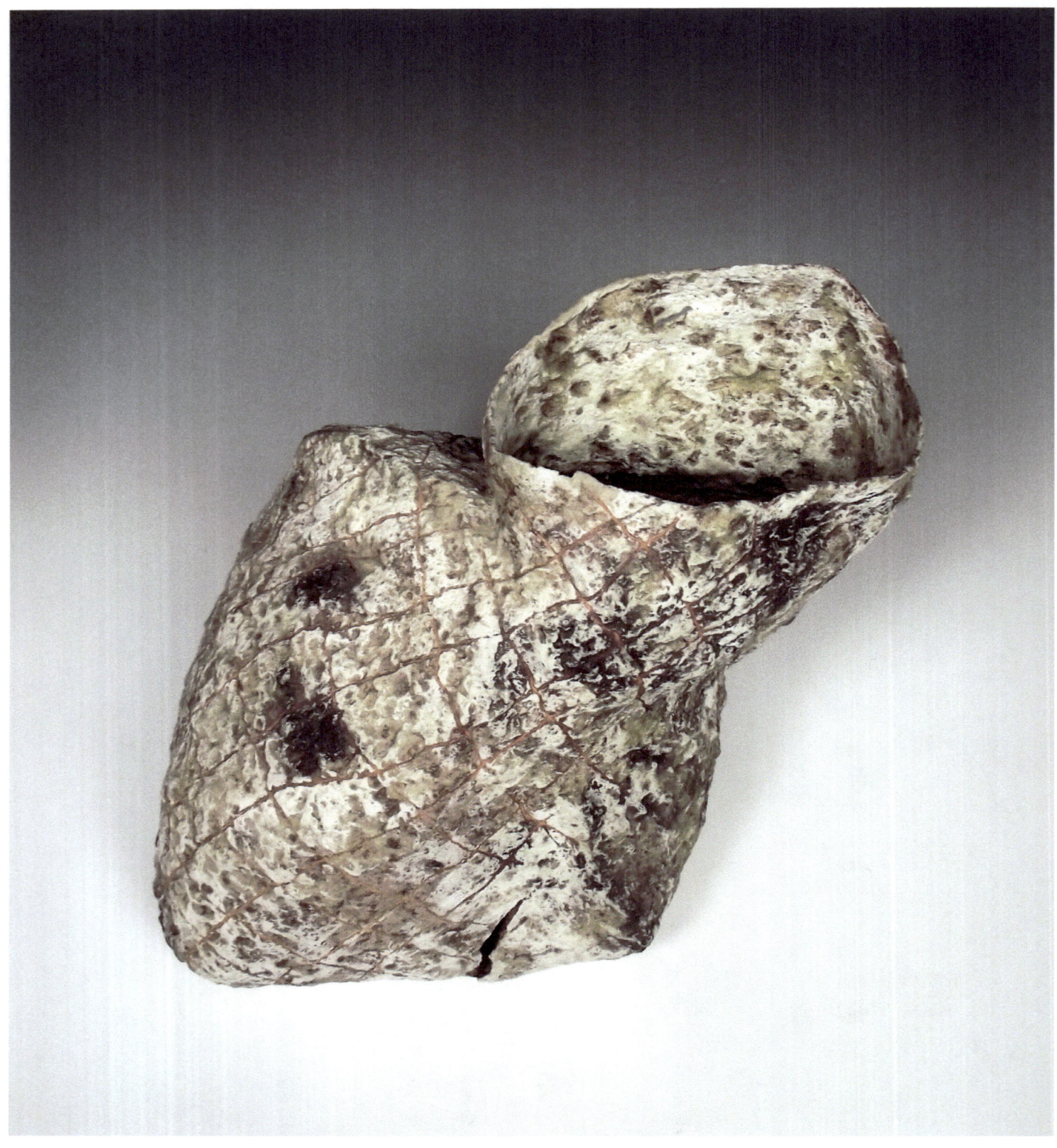

Previous page spread, left & right:

Ewen Henderson, (1934-2000)
Sculptural Vessel, 20th Century
Collection of Diane & Igal Silber

Henry Pim, (b. 1947)
Sculptural Vessel, 20th Century
Collection of Lynn Myers

Sara Radstone, (b. 1955)
Sculptural Form, 1984
Collection of Diane & Igal Silber

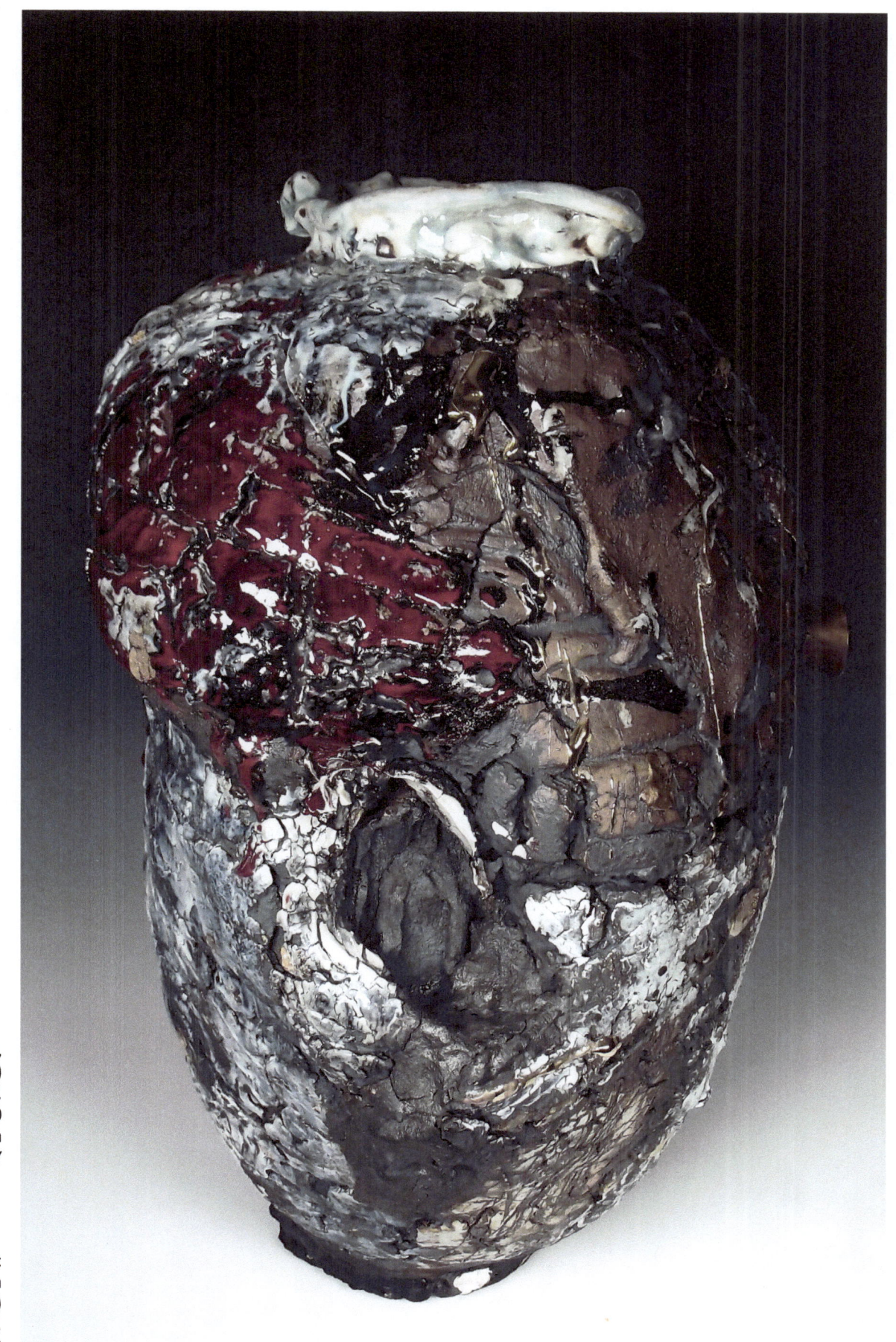

Gareth Mason,
(b. 1965)
Sculptural Vessel,
c. 2000
Courtesy of Jason
Jacques Gallery, NY

Back Cover:
Gareth Mason
(b. 1965)
Sculptural Vessel,
c. 2000
Collection of Judy
and Richard Jacobs